Buddhist-Christian Dialogue, U.S. Law, and Womanist Theology for Transgender Spiritual Care

"Writing with a theologian's heart, a lawyer's mind, and a bodhisattva's compas sion, Yetunde identifies the constitutional and legal literacies chaplains can develop to help protect the civil and religious rights of trans people as they are deliberately erased and exposed to harm by the Religious Right in collusion with the Trump regime. The book makes important contributions to spiritual care for trans communities and to the emerging pastoral literature of Buddhist-Christian studies".

—Duane Bidwell, *Professor of Practical Theology, Spiritual Care, and Counseling, Claremont School of Theology* and author of *When One Religion Isn't Enough: The Lives of Spiritually Fluid People* (2018)

"Integrating passionate socio-political engagement and legal acumen with spiritual insight from Buddhist and Christian traditions, the author makes a convincing case for welcoming and full inclusion of the vulnerable among us who tend to be despised by many in society, making an appeal for disobedience, resistance, and eventual transformation of oppressive laws designed to exclude 'the least of these (Mt. 25:40)'".

—Ruben L. F. Habito, *Professor of World Religions and Spirituality, Perkins School of Theology, Southern Methodist University* and author of *Be Still and Know: Zen and the Bible* (2017)

Pamela Ayo Yetunde

Buddhist-Christian Dialogue, U.S. Law, and Womanist Theology for Transgender Spiritual Care

palgrave
macmillan

Pamela Ayo Yetunde
United Theological Seminary of the Twin Cities
St. Paul, MN, USA

Upaya Institute and Zen Center
Santa Fe, NM, USA

ISBN 978-3-030-42559-3   ISBN 978-3-030-42560-9   (eBook)
https://doi.org/10.1007/978-3-030-42560-9

This Palgrave Pivot imprint is published by the registered company Springer Nature
Switzerland AG.
The registered company address is: Gewerbestrasse 11, 6330 Cham, Switzerland

Dedicated to all people trying to be who they truly are.

ACKNOWLEDGMENTS

Gratitude is a spiritual practice that leads directly to happiness. Dependent origination and interdependence are concepts that explain how nothing arises by itself and how everything is dependent on other phenomena. That is to say, I am going to thank several people and institutions for supporting me on this project, and their support is dependent on causes and conditions not mentioned in these few words of acknowledgment. I want to thank United Theological Seminary of the Twin Cities for granting me leave to conduct research and Dr. Cheryl A. Giles, Psy.D., for inviting me to Harvard Divinity School's Post-Doctoral Fellowship Program. Dr. Giles's mentorship was beyond compare. I'm grateful to John Freese, Rev. Margo Richardson, La Sarmiento, Rev. Vicki Richardson, Lucia Kalinosky, Rev. Liam Muggleton Robins, ACPE Educator, Interfaith Minister, Transgender (this is how Liam identifies themselves), Cheri Ho, A. J. Johnston, Rev. Peter Bauck, and Lama Rod Owens for reading portions of my manuscript. Thank you to Rev. Dr. Jennie Gould and Dr. Jennifer Siegel at Boston Medical Center for allowing me to interview them during times that were perhaps extraordinarily busy for them. I want to thank Chaplain LaTonya Davis, who contributed feedback to my other book, *Object Relations, Buddhism, and Womanist Practical Theology* (Palgrave Macmillan). Thank you to Aurora Jade Pichette, Nate Metrick, and Jake Bradley, experts in the areas of transgender people, religion, and pastoral care, who I met at the 2018 Parliament of the World's Religions in Toronto. I am grateful for Palgrave Macmillan and Amy Invernizzi, who shepherded both of my books with timeliness and ease, and editor Katy Klutznick for pulling my manuscript together. Thank you Hemalatha Arumugam for the ease your brought to the production process. Lastly, I want to thank Tracey Scott for the freedom she allows in our relationship, for making space for me to leave and return.

CONTENTS

Buddhist-Christian Interreligious Dialogue for Spiritual Care for Transgender Hospital Patients

Abstract The Pastoral Care profession in public hospitals in the United States has been largely populated and led by Protestant Christians. Buddhist practitioners have entered the field creating opportunities for Christian-Buddhist dialogue. Transgender US citizens are especially vulnerable to medical, social, and spiritual neglect in health care settings due to policy changes in the Department of Health and Human Services. Christians are also vulnerable to the manipulation of basic Christian principles by Trump and Pence. Buddhist-Christian dialogue can strengthen compassionate care and promote public practical theology for transgender hospital patients.

Keywords Buddhist • Christian • Transgender • Interreligious Dialogue • Law

INTRODUCTION

First they came for the socialists, and I did not speak out—
Because I was not a socialist.
Then they came for the trade unionists, and I did not speak out—
Because I was not a trade unionist.
Then they came for the Jews, and I did not speak out—

© The Author(s) 2020
P. A. Yetunde, *Buddhist-Christian Dialogue, U.S. Law, and Womanist Theology for Transgender Spiritual Care,*
https://doi.org/10.1007/978-3-030-42560-9_1

1

> *Because I was not a Jew.*
> *Then they came for me—and there was no one left to speak for me.*
> Lutheran pastor Martin Niemoller

Prescript. Years before I began writing this book, I anticipated President Trump would be impeached. He was impeached on December 18, 2019. COVID-19 was reported to the World Health Organization in late December of that year. Trump was acquitted on February 5, 2020, as the COVID-19 pandemic continued ravaging humanity. Before attention was paid to Trump's dealings with Ukraine, and before COVID-19 reared its ugly head, our government targeted transgender people in nearly every facet and sector of American life. At the time of writing, COVID-19 is demanding something different from us—a political system that is transparent, responsive to public health concerns, economically nimble, and ceases the targeting of politically-vulnerable citizens. At this time, governments across the globe are aware of the desperate necessity of garnering nearly every possible resource to protect humanity from the scourge of the coronavirus. No country will "go it alone" and thrive. Communicable diseases remind us that we are all in this together, and spiritual care providers must attend to political situations outside our clinical contexts. What happens outside impacts what happens inside. Medical professionals (many of whom are wearing garbage bags for protective gear) are putting their lives as risk, and some are dying. This is a tragedy and travesty. Impeachment reminds us that the President is accountable to the US Constitution and Trump's acquittal reminds us that in this Administration, foreign nationals are invited to meddle in our electoral processes without real consequence. Moreover, I hope these situations remind us, intergenerationally, that our survival as a species depends on recognizing and honoring our interdependence across gender, gender expression, sex, sexuality, sexual expressions, and all forms of human expression. This is what the Parable of the Good Samaritan or the Parable of Our Collective Survival, teaches us. Are we ready to learn?

Chaplains. We love chaplains who nonjudgmentally support us in times of need, often in places we don't wish to be, or places we have a difficult time adjusting to. They represent the kinds of people Jesus talked about in The Parable of the Good Samaritan. Millions of Americans receive their *primary* spiritual care from "good Samaritan" chaplains,[1] but chaplains are not known for collectively speaking out on behalf of the oppressed. I argue that pastoral and spiritual caregivers need to be involved in democratic institutions beyond voting; as educated, critically thinking spiritual leaders they hold the potential to wisely engage in the democratic process in ways that can contribute wisdom and compassion in the protection of minority rights while respecting religious freedom. Unfortunately, many spiritual care professionals are not prepared for such critical involvement because seminary education and Clinical Pastoral Education (CPE) are typically not infused with legal education. How might chaplains, spiritual caregivers, pastoral counselors, and chaplain educators with some education in US religious freedom law read Christian scriptures differently? More importantly, how might these spiritual caregivers and educators act differently?

Lawyers. We love lawyers when they successfully defend our rights; we hate them when they successfully defend the rights of someone suing or prosecuting us. Human rights lawyers are known for speaking out on behalf of the oppressed, but are not known for collectively offering spiritual care to those who are sick. Though this book is not written for lawyers, how might lawyers interpret laws differently, as the lawyer learned to do in his encounter with Jesus, if those interpretations were made with the sensibility of a spiritual caregiver?

Sagacious mystics. Everyone loves the wise person who sees us for who we truly are, without judgment, and who takes the time to direct our attention toward what is good. These people may irritate us when they puncture our egos, reminding us that we are not as great as we might imagine, and when they point out unseen forces in the universe greater than ourselves. They help us see beyond the mundane and they illuminate the sublime. Sagacious mystics, unlike chaplains and lawyers, tend to transcend professional categorization and do not separate their wisdom from their identities and their behavior. Scripture, law, and being are one.

So, what happens when the incisive lawyer confronts the mystical sage with questions about the rule of law and salvation, and the sage replies that caring for others is the path? This kind of confrontation unfolds in one of the most powerfully humanizing stories of all time: The Parable of the Good Samaritan (The Parable); but The Parable is under attack in the United States, especially with respect to transgender people. Why is it that a powerfully humanizing narrative would be intentionally threatened?

In the Christian Bible, in the Gospel of Luke, a lawyer asks Jesus what he must do in order to live forever. Jesus asks him how he interprets the law. The lawyer understands the law in this way: One must love God with every fiber of one's being and love one's neighbor as one loves oneself. Jesus affirms the lawyer's understanding. Digging deeper, as good lawyers tend to do, the lawyer asks for Jesus's definition of the word "neighbor." Jesus tells the lawyer a story, a parable, about a man who is severely beaten and left for dead, even by religious leaders who see the dying man and cross to the other side of the road. A Samaritan, someone not esteemed in any religious or ethnic way, a commoner, perhaps even someone oppressed, gives the dying man aid and takes him to an inn for care. He pays the innkeeper, offering to pay even more than requested. The innkeeper takes the man into his care. After Jesus tells the story, he turns the question back on the lawyer, asking for his definition of the word "neighbor." The lawyer responds by equating the word neighbor with the Samaritan—a neighbor is one who shows mercy, as the Samaritan showed mercy upon the dying man. Jesus affirms the answer and instructs the lawyer to do likewise.[2] We do not know the end of the story; we don't discover how the lawyer enacts or does not enact Jesus's instruction. We do, however, know the story of a challenge to Jesus's message, a challenge that is taking place in contemporary America. The Trump-Pence administration, in the name of Christianity, is currently flouting the Good Samaritan ethos. Why?

Prior to the 2016 presidential election in the United States, real-estate mogul and presidential candidate Donald J. Trump, with celebrity status and wealth but without a strong political base, struck a deal with some politicized and energized Christian evangelicals. These evangelicals sought political access and power they certainly would not have found with Trump's opponent, liberal Protestant, feminist Hillary Rodham Clinton, a former first lady, US Senator, and secretary of state. Though candidate Trump did not espouse discrimination against transgender citizens in the presidential debates, the base brought their anti-LGBTQ and especially their anti-transgender agenda to his presidency. With the help of Russian meddling in social media and voting systems, Trump, despite his non-Christian lifestyle, became the darling of some Christian evangelicals, not to mention some African-American Christian pastors and many white nationalists, some of whom were and are in the Trump-Pence administration. Politics makes for strange bedfellows.

Trump entered the presidency on January 20, 2017. Just shy of a month in office, his administration eliminated federal protections that allowed transgender students to use bathrooms consistent with their gender identity.[3] About one year later, President Trump said on Religious Freedom Day,

Our Constitution and laws guarantee Americans the right not just to believe as they see fit, but to freely exercise their religion. … No American—whether a nun, nurse, baker, or business owner—should be forced to choose between the tenets of faith or adherence to the law.[4]

A Christian nun would not struggle between the tenets of her faith and The Parable, because The Parable is a part of her faith. A nurse would not struggle between The Parable and their profession, because The Parable is part of their profession. Through the equal protection clause of the Fourteenth Amendment, this country seeks to ensure that all citizens are treated as endowed with the same substance, thereby recognizing that no one is better than or more entitled to rights than anyone else. Under the Fourteenth Amendment, bakers and other business owners offering their services and products to the public may not deny their services and products to different classes of people; but that is indeed happening, and it is happening legally. The Parable is under attack in the name of religious freedom, but the Good Samaritans in our midst can use the power of the principle to re-imagine The Parable beyond its focus on the goodness of one human toward another human. I will return to the process of this re-imaging in Chap. 6.

The Parable is being twisted, civility is being undermined, and compassion is being devalued. As the gender-bending rock star David Bowie sang in lamentation about political corruption,

This is not America … A little piece of you
The little peace in me
Will die
For this is not America[5]

The small pieces of peace within our hearts that have been cultivated by The Parable are dying as transgender US citizens are being sacrificed on the political altar. All the while, The Parable teaches us not to make others vulnerable and not to exacerbate the vulnerability of those who are struggling to survive.

As I watched the 2016 presidential debates, when candidate Trump initially had no discernable political base, I saw from the outside the development of his relationship with former Indiana Governor Mike Pence and Pence-style Christians. In short, Pence-style Christians believe in a Christianity that is more biblically literal, believe God is judgmental and damning, and believe in separating "sinners" from the "saved." They do not believe in the separation of church and state; arguably, they believe in church *as* state. The failed attempt to adopt a radically discriminatory Religious Freedom Restoration Act (discussed in more detail in Chap. 4) in Indiana demonstrates this assertion. How can the twisting and destruction of The Parable occur in a country where many hospitals throughout the country are named "Good Samaritan" and where we continue to celebrate Good Samaritan acts in the news? This is not America. Or, is it?

Our organizing principles of compassion and mercy are obviously fragile. For as we have seen in a short period of time, the very possibility of human flourishing among millions of Americans can be undermined by religious prejudices, laws, and policies that change with radical changes in the political situation.

The US transgender community is under attack in nearly every sector of society by its own federal government, nominally in the interest of protecting the religious freedom of anti-trans people to discriminate. My theological formation in womanist practical theology informs my ethic of creating safe spaces for everyone, including transgender people. This womanist safe-space sensitivity helps me see that the US public health care system is being impoverished through the Conscience and Religious Freedom Division (CRFD) of the Department of Health and Human Services—in the interest of protecting the religious freedom to discriminate. African-American theologically educated political scientist, author, television host, and advocate Melissa Harris-Perry's work inspires me to say something, write something, and do something about the religion-fueled human rights situation before us because transgender people are under siege in the Trump-Pence administration. Harris-Perry, though not considered by many to be a theologian per se, advocates in a theologically sophisticated, compelling, and multi-faceted manner for sexuality-oppressed people. She is an inspiration for chaplains and spiritual care professionals seeking to take their ministries of compassion to the streets, within the academy, and throughout the airwaves. As a political scientist, she is also an exemplar for public practical theological leadership. Leadership matters. Where transgender rights were emerging in schools, public restrooms, the military, and in health care under the Obama Administration, the Trump-Pence administration in short order repealed and attempted to repeal regulations that supported trans people in schools, employment, housing, health care, and the military.

According to The National Center for Transgender Equality, these are some actions, in various sectors of society, that have been taken against transgender citizens:

March 2017: The Department of Housing and Urban Development (HUD) removed links to four key resource documents from its website, which informed emergency shelters on best practices for serving transgender people facing homelessness and complying with HUD regulations.

March 28, 2017: The Census Bureau retracted a proposal to collect demographic information on LGBT people in the 2020 Census.

March 31, 2017: The Justice Department announced it would review (and likely seek to scale back) numerous civil rights settlement agreements with police departments. These settlements were put in places where police departments were determined to be engaging in discriminatory and abusive policing, including racial and other profiling. Many of these agreements include critical protections for LGBT people.

April 4, 2017: The Justice and Labor Departments cancelled quarterly conference calls with LGBT organizations; on these calls, which have happened for years, government attorneys share information on employment laws and cases.

October 5, 2017: The Justice Department released a memo instructing Department of Justice attorneys to take the legal position that federal law does not protect transgender workers from discrimination.

October 6, 2017: The Justice Department released a sweeping "license to discriminate," allowing federal agencies, government contractors, government grantees, and even private businesses to engage in illegal discrimination, as long as they can cite religious reasons for doing so.

December 14, 2017: Staff at the Centers for Disease Control and Prevention were instructed not to use the words "transgender," "vulnerable," "entitlement," "diversity," "fetus," "evidence-based," and "science-based" in official documents.

January 18, 2018: The Department of Health and Human Services Office for Civil Rights opened a "Conscience and Religious Freedom Division" that will promote discrimination by health care providers who can cite religious or moral reasons for denying care. (I return to this subject in Chap. 4.)

January 26, 2018: The Department of Health and Human Services proposed a rule that encourages religious refusals in health care targeting trans people, people who need reproductive care, and others.

February 18, 2018: The Department of Education announced it will summarily dismiss complaints from transgender students involving exclusion from school facilities and other claims based solely on gender identity discrimination.

March 23, 2018: The Trump administration announced an implementation plan for its discriminatory ban on transgender military service members.

May 11, 2018: The Bureau of Prisons in the Department of Justice adopted an illegal policy of almost entirely housing transgender people in federal prison facilities that match their sex assigned at birth, rolling back existing protections.

August 10, 2018: The Department of Labor released a new directive for Office of Federal Contract Compliance Programs (OFCCP) staff, encouraging them to grant broad religious exemptions to federal contractors with religious-based objections to complying with nondiscrimination laws. It also deleted material from an OFCCP frequently asked questions on LGBT nondiscrimination protections that had previously clarified the limited scope of allowable religious exemptions.[6]

Since this list was compiled, in October 2018, it was leaked to the press that the Trump-Pence administration would strike the category of transgender people from Title IX legislation.[7] In January 2019, the Trump-Pence administration won a federal court legal victory against trans people with a gender dysphoria diagnosis, barring them from military service.[8]

If the Parable of the Good Samaritan is part of Christian teachings and part of our national values, then these Christians are actively paving the path to hell by making health care clinics, hospice organizations, hospitals, and so on, places where transgender people (and others) can be refused care, even by spiritual care and medical professionals, on religious grounds. These governmental-based discriminatory policies extend beyond health care to various sectors of society. Is this a perversion of Christianity? Why should I, a cisgender person, care?

The first transgender person I met was my mother's colleague, a federal employee, who was transitioning from male to female in Indianapolis in the early 1980s. My mother explained that even though neither of us understood what "Tom" was going through, I should still respect her. My mother had demonstrated throughout her life that being a good friend to all enriches life. Since meeting Tom, I have come into contact with many people who experience gender in a variety of ways. In the early 1990s, a prospective financial planning client of mine transitioned from being a woman to being a man. One of my first pastoral counseling clients was a trans woman. A friend with whom I completed Buddhist leadership training identifies as genderqueer. I served on a panel with someone who was gender nonconforming and is now a man. I worked with a mental health care intern who had transitioned from woman to man. One morning while walking into the front door of the seminary where I teach, I met a lesbian couple that had been evicted from a Christian shelter for homeless people because one of the women was trans and wanted to use the women's restroom. I have provided pastoral counseling to clients who have transitioned from one gender to another, and now I have an esteemed seminary professor colleague with whom I have a collaborative relationship.

I have learned, since the mid-1980s, in different contexts and in different parts of the country, that no matter one's gender assignment at birth, gender alone does not define a person; a change in gender does not negate an individual's personhood.

I am not an expert on what it means to be a transgender person, nor am I an expert in transgender spiritual care. My trans and religious conversation partners, Aurora Jade Pichette (www.jadepichette.com), and Jake Bradley and Nate Metrick of Elements Consulting (www.elementsconsulting.org), are the experts. My expertise, as a law-educated, womanist-inspired practical theologian educated in spiritually integrated Marriage and Family Therapy, is in seeing how religious freedom laws are intentionally distorted to negatively impact transgender people while they are seeking health care. This book is offered as a resource for inspiring chaplains and spiritual caregivers in hospitals to widen the field of spiritual care for trans hospital patients by undergoing our own transitioning: away from leaving religious freedom law literacy in the hands of lawyers exclusively; away from religious monologue and toward interreligious dialogue; and away from exclusivist private, patient-centered care toward public, hospital-communal care. Changes in the White House demand that we increase our vigilance toward the care of others by speaking publicly about oppression.

My mother raised me to care about the well-being of people, the planet, and the universe and its inhabitants. We share a cosmic home with countless species. I am not a transgender person, but I believe that if I were, my fundamental desires would remain the same: love, respect, safety, compassion, empathy, work, fun, housing, an education, freedom, faith, family, and health care. I do not locate myself entirely within Christian devotion and worship. I define myself as an interfaith Buddhist practitioner. I was raised in the United Methodist Church, worked abroad and stateside as a Church of the Brethren volunteer, attended a silent Quaker Meeting for some years, attended an Episcopal Church for some years, and a Lutheran Adult Sunday School. I was introduced to Buddhism through

Thich Nhat Hanh's writings, the Zen Hospice Project where I volunteered, the Community of Mindful Living sanghas in the San Francisco East Bay, and Spirit Rock Meditation Center. I still embrace the Jesus-Christian ethos in which I was reared. I eventually entered and withdrew from leadership training in the Community of Mindful Living and entered and completed leadership training in Spirit Rock's Community Dharma Leaders program. I earned a master's degree at a Catholic University and a doctor of theology degree from a Presbyterian seminary. I have a law degree from a state university.

Through my travels through religious and spiritual traditions and communities, I have come to love a broad range of scriptures that arise out of various traditions, from The Gospels to *The Way of the Bodhisattva* to the *Daode jing* to the *Bhagavad Gita*. I see myself as a witness to the suffering we inflict upon one another. I am convinced that through spiritual practice, we can learn to treat one another better than we do.

Christianity teaches me about loving my neighbor as I love myself. Buddhism teaches me how to understand suffering, my own and another's, without sliding into despair, with a willingness and capacity to be present and appropriate. Christianity teaches me to be an advocate and Buddhism teaches me to take care of myself as I advocate for others. Neither tradition helps me to understand trans people specifically (though there are teachings that are helpful), and neither tradition has fully prepared me for examining what it will take for health care organizations in an increasingly fascist-leaning Executive Office (the abuse of our democratic institutions by neglect, the demonization and of the press and vilification of journalists, autocracy, the emboldening of hate groups, and the intimidation of resistance movements), to intentionally become hospitable toward transgender people. Supported by Christianity and Buddhism, I wish to forge a new path toward understanding and welcoming all people who are vulnerable in this particularly destructive political moment in the United States.

Being hospitable is a value shared by all major religious traditions, including Buddhism, Christianity, Hinduism, Islam, and Judaism; being hospitable, or having the ability to be a host, is the very action out of which hospitals and hospices were originally founded. The word "hospital" is derived from "ospital," meaning, "hostel, shelter, lodging."[9] Indeed, churches and religious organizations were the first creators of hospitals, which were primarily intended for serving poor people.[10]

Chaplains serve as hosts in hospitals and hospices; they provide hospitality in the form of religious and spiritual support, when requested. In *A Ministry of Presence: Chaplaincy, Spiritual Care, and the Law,* Winnifred Fallers Sullivan offers that chaplains are "trained by religious communities [to] minister to a clientele often unmarked at that moment by any specific religious identity, and they do so on behalf of a secular institution bound, at least theoretically, to rational epistemologies. ... The chaplain has, without paradox, become a priest of the secular ... attempt[ing] to integrate universalist and particularist understandings of the flourishing of human beings under the banner of religious freedom."[11]

Sullivan also claims, "The new 'clinical' chaplaincy has a different role and a different purpose. The chaplain has now become a member of the medical team."[12] Consequently, as a member of the medical team, utilizing a ministry of presence,

> Each [chaplain] experiences the intimate and immediate face of death and dying and the insistent presence of difficult moral decisions. But they share much with other forms of chaplaincy today. The diversity of their clientele, the ambiguity of lines of authority, the transience of the encounter, and, above all, the pressure to work in a radically undefined setting religiously speaking, and a rapidly deconstructing religious field—while justifying that work using the seductively scientistic language of spiritual assessment and care—characterizes the work that chaplains do in every place. Chaplains are at a particularly interesting and focused interface between church, state, society, and a rapidly changing religious terrain.[13]

Due to the fact that chaplains are educated in, exposed to, and trained in a variety of disciplines, including theology and critical analysis of sacred texts, professional chaplains know that interpreting The Parable *against* vulnerable patients is a gross perversion. The US Department of Health and Human Services (HHS) created an Office for Civil Rights (OCR) enforcement mechanism called the Conscience and Religious Freedom Division (CRFD) to enable health care employees to file complaints online if they cannot remove themselves from caring for people they do not like, in the name of religion. It is estimated that this initiative will cost hundreds of millions of dollars every year. It is estimated that the cost to implement CRFD is $900,000, that it will cost $312.3 million this year, and $125.5 million every year. Are our health care systems able to survive such financial losses?[14] The Trump-Pence administration is also promoting vigilante justice by inviting people to file complaints on another's behalf without their knowledge or permission. Can you image, for example, a member of a religion that despises white people removing herself from caring for all white patients in a hospital? Should she be entitled to keep her job? Can you imagine a white hospice worker belonging to a religion that espouses white supremacy removing himself from the care of all people of color? Can you imagine a Jewish health care clinic employee who believes that neo-Nazis should not be provided treatment because they advocate violence having the right to refuse to provide care? Should a Roman Catholic priest who is a chaplain be able to exercise his religious freedom by performing an exorcism on anyone he deems in need? Whether it is the individual hospital, hospice, or clinic employee with their particular belief systems encountering individual patients who fall outside the net of love and compassion of their religious, spiritual, and ethical systems, should the entire hospital, hospice, or clinic be denied federal funding based on those religious differences?

Should the United States, with a Constitutional mandate in the First Amendment to keep church and state separate, be involved in withholding necessary funds for sites of hospitality, based on religious disputes within those organizations? It is important to note here that though the founding fathers were stricter regarding the separation of church and state, over time, and especially recently, the US Supreme Court has been more liberal on questions of religion-state relationships. Sullivan says,

> Decisions of the U.S. Supreme Court in the last couple of decades have shifted the Court's interpretation of the religion clauses of the First Amendment away from the high separationism of the middle part of the twentieth century toward a jurisprudence that increasingly sees religion as being neither particularly threatening nor particularly in need of protection.[15]

Is this neutral attitude shifting more toward protection? As it relates to the executive branch, there is a clear shift toward protection through the Trump-Pence administration's Conscience and Religious Freedom Division.

As a practical theologian, one who has worked in hospice, hospital, and mental health care settings, I want to know how to remedy the things that have become so wrong, especially for transgender people. In the Gospel of Matthew, Jesus says, "Truly I tell you, whatever you did for one of *the least of these* [italics mine] brothers and sisters of mine, you did for me." Biblical literalists, ready for a self-righteous argument, may pounce on Jesus's words, saying, "See, it says 'brothers and sisters,' not transgender people." Who could disagree? The incisive lawyer in The Parable, who questions Jesus about the definition of the word "neighbor," might ask, "What is a brother? What is a sister? What do we call people who don't identify as either? If I do for the least of these, those who are neither, am I also doing for Jesus?" When taking scripture literally, we become spiritually stuck in bibliolatry—making the Bible an idol of worship. The lawyer questioning Jesus and Jesus sharing The Parable serves as an interrelational dynamic for avoiding bibliolatry; the lawyer, who was capable of reading and understanding the law as it was written, was yet in need of guidance from a wise mystic.

Wise mysticism helps us see what is not obvious to the naked eye. Wise mysticism helps us understand our place in the cosmos, levels our egos, and transforms negative perceptions, enabling us to see beyond delusions, delusions that include how we may view trans people, whether they are represented in our sacred texts or not. The wise mystic in us might answer the incisive lawyer in us by saying, "The least of us is never determined based upon gender identification only, but on vulnerability and need, and we are always subject to vulnerability and need." A common person of no religious title or position, perhaps no religious belief and certainly vulnerable and in need, can still do for the least of these. How might we go forth and do so without explicit guidance from our ancient scriptures?

Being transgender, as we understand it today, rests outside many ancient sacred texts. For Bible literalists, there is no mention of what we should do for Jesus if we encounter someone who was a brother but is now a sister, was a sister but is now a brother, or someone who is not a sister or a brother, yet is still a person. Yet, reading the Gospels in their entirety, it is reasonable to imagine that anyone who is "the least of these" and is given aide by another will share some of the spiritual substance of Jesus's substance—an enlightening spirituality. This enlightening spirituality is what I call The Christ and from a Buddhist perspective, The Tathagata (subjects I discuss in Chaps. 1 and 3). I am suggesting that the concept of The Christ and the concept of The Tathagata overlap and provide an interreligious bridge of understanding, compassion, and action for the benefit of the clinical spiritual care of transgender people now under attack through the auspices of the Department of Health and Human Services' Conscience and Religious Freedom Division.

Transgender people are targeted by the federal government from a multitude of directions, in all places, regardless of age and ability, in society at large, in family at small, and oftentimes intrapsychically due to multidimensional societal invalidation. No ancient religious text directly and explicitly prepares us for deeming transgender people fully human and worthy of respect in the material world if we already have a notion that aligning one's body with one's persistent thoughts about oneself is wrong. How many people have dyed their hair in an effort to look younger when in the material world, we do not actually get younger? How many people have had plastic surgery in an effort to maintain a youthful appearance when we do not "age in place?" How many women have had medical procedures in order to have children? How many men take erectile dysfunction medication past their sexual prime? Trans people are not the only people who take measures to align their bodies with their self-concepts, and that is important to note as we move toward the recognition that we share the desire to feel and be whole and not be discriminated against just because we are making these decisions. It is the recognition that we human beings desire to feel and be whole that forms the ground for revitalizing and re-imagining The Parable of the Good Samaritan as The Parable for Our Collective Survival.

The revitalization and re-imagining of The Parable arguably begins with Chap. 1, "Buddhist-Christian Interreligious Dialogue for Spiritual Care for Transgender Hospital Patients," where I introduce ways for Buddhist and Christian spiritual caregivers to engage in interreligious dialogue and cooperation to expand the field and scope of care within the hospital context as well as how to enter Buddhist dialogue with Christians, especially as it relates to St. Paul's letters to the Galatians and Colossians about "identity disformation" in Jesus Christ. In Chap. 2, "Spiritual Care and Political Involvement, Womanist Public Theology and Boston Medical Center," I utilize the life and work of black feminist, womanist-influenced, African-American public intellectual Melissa Harris-Perry to illustrate how one might engage citizenship through being a scholar, a journalist, an advocate, and a theologian. In Chap. 2, I also examine and analyze the data from three surveys—one with chaplains, one with pastoral counselors, and the other with chaplain educators—all related to religious freedom issues, spiritual care, and education. I conducted these surveys to arrive at a sense of what some chaplains, pastoral counselors, and chaplain educators really think about religious freedom law and determine if CPE programs incorporate religious freedom law literacy in their curricula. In addition to the surveys, I include a brief case study on the Clinical Pastoral Education program at Boston Medical Center's Center for Transgender Medicine and Surgery. In Chap. 3, "Thich Nhat Hanh, the Avatamsaka Sutra, and Lady Mahamaya," I introduce Vietnamese Zen Buddhist monk Thich Nhat Hanh's teachings on the *Avatamsaka Sutra* and, more specifically, on Lady Mahamaya, the Buddha's mother. Hanh's cosmic Zen Buddhism promotes the notions of emptiness, impermanence, and interdependency, even as it relates to gender. Nhat Hanh's cosmic Buddhology offers "intelligent design" Christians engaged in interreligious dialogue with Buddhists, mystical wisdom and spiritual practices to consider when contemplating deepening empathy with transgender hospital patients. In Chap. 4, "Think Like a Lawyer, Act Like a Chaplain," I examine issues related to the US Constitution, case law, and state legislation related to religious freedom and spiritual care. In Chap. 5, "A New 'Shock Method' for Creating a Compassionate Health Care Team," I introduce a combination of methods for widening the field and scope of spiritual care for trans hospital patients through the writings of black, Buddhist, queer activists Rev. angel Kyodo williams, Lama Rod Owens, Professor Jasmine Syedullah, and Christian pastoral theologian Brita Gill-Austern. In Chap. 6, "Conclusions and Recommendations," I offer concluding remarks, recommendations, and a vitally important reinterpretation of The Parable of the Good Samaritan for our collective survival.

All, too, will bear in mind this sacred principle, that though the will of the majority is in all cases to prevail, that will to be rightful must be reasonable; that the minority possess their equal rights, which equal law must protect, and to violate would be oppression.
Thomas Jefferson

Most Christian 'believers' tend to echo the cultural prejudices and worldviews of the dominant group in their country, with only a minority revealing any real transformation of attitudes or consciousness. It has been true of slavery and racism, classism and consumerism and issues of immigration and health care for the poor.
Richard Rohr

One of my messages to Republicans is very simple: One-third of your schedule should be listening to people in minority communities.
Newt Gingrich[16]

Philosopher Craig Calhoun says,

> Religion is threatening, inspiring, consoling, provocative, a matter of reassuring routine or calls to put one's life on the line. It is a way to make peace and a reason to make war. As the great Iranian sociologist and Islamic reformer Ali Sharyati put it: "Religion is an amazing phenomenon that plays contradictory roles in people's lives. It can destroy or revitalize, put to sleep or awaken, enslave or emancipate, teach docility or teach revolt." No wonder debates about religion in the public sphere can be so confusing.[17]

The multiple and conflicting potentialities and impacts of religion in the US's pluralistic and democratic society necessitates chaplains and spiritual caregivers being deeply engaged in interreligious dialogue and public advocacy for the oppressed in order for us to survive as whole beings in a whole nation, contributing to a whole continent and world. When I think about interreligious dialogue, I imagine two parties from different religious traditions engaged with each other on matters vital to their religious belief systems, with the knowledge that the other possesses different beliefs, with a desire to know the other more deeply in order to cohabitate more peaceably. Judith Butler writes about cohabitation, specifically in the Israel-Palestine context:

> Cohabitation forms the ethical basis for a public critique of those forms of state violence that seek to produce and maintain the Jewish character of the state through the radical disenfranchisement and decimation of its minority, through occupation, assault, or legal restriction. These are attacks on a subjugated minority, but they are also attacks on the value of cohabitation.[18]

The Trump-Pence administration's systematic attack on transgender people is an attack on cohabitation—by the power of religious freedom, we have been given a "license to prey" on transgender citizens through discrimination in housing, the workplace, education, the military, and elsewhere. Butler's cohabitation concept is complex and beyond the once-popular question, "Can't we all just get along?" posed by Rodney King, an African-American man who was brutally beaten by police in 1991. Butler is talking about the fact that we cannot choose who inhabits this planet without committing acts of genocide. The fact that we cannot choose who inhabits the planet without committing acts of genocide informs us of a variety of moral options and ethical dilemmas before us.

One of those moral options is respecting the fact that others value the traditions they identify with. Vietnamese Buddhist monk Thich Nhat Hanh writes,

> Sharing [interreligious dialogue] in this way is important and should be encouraged. But sharing does not mean wanting others to abandon their own spiritual roots and embrace your faith. That would be cruel. People are stable and happy only when they are firmly rooted in their own tradition and culture. To uproot them would make them suffer.[19]

Nhat Hanh seems to support the notion of cohabitation by suggesting that people should be able to maintain the strength of their "spiritual roots" while engaging in interreligious dialogue. However, in clinical settings, we are all rooted in one vast space that houses a multitude of individuals rooted in different beliefs and traditions. How do we work within these tensions in a balanced way?

In chaplaincy training, chaplain educators instruct their students in clinical settings where they encounter patients from all walks of life, with a variety of illnesses, undergoing a variety of procedures, and encountering a variety of professionals. Chaplaincy students, if they are fortunate, enter into a clinical setting with other students from different religions and worldviews. If their fortune is extended, the other students will be from different cultures, nations, age groups, sexualities, and gender expressions. Great fortune is had if the student has a chaplain educator who embraces and even represents diversity and plurality.

In this chapter, I draw on Christian theologian Paul O. Ingram's *The Process of Buddhist-Christian Dialogue*, discussing ways Buddhists and Christians working together as chaplains and chaplain students in hospitals can contribute to hate-proofing their hospitals on behalf of trans patients. I will also build on Ingram's processes to offer additional perspectives on how Buddhist-Christian dialogue in the hospital context for spiritual care for trans patients might be achieved. But before engaging Ingram, it is important to note that interreligious dialogue will not occur on any deep psychologically transformative level if dialogue partners are so narcissistically impaired as to prohibit deep listening, empathy, and authentic consideration of others. Nhat Hanh says,

> In true dialogue, both sides are willing to change. We have to appreciate that truth can be received from outside of—not only within—our own

group. Dialogue is not a means for assimilation in the sense that one side expands and incorporates the other into its "self." Dialogue must be practiced on the basis of "non-self."[20]

"Non-self" in this context is defined as not afflicted with Narcissistic Personality Disorder (NDP), which is,

A pervasive pattern of grandiosity (in fantasy or behavior), need for admiration, and lack of empathy, beginning by early adulthood and present in a variety of contexts, as indicated by five (or more) of the following:

1. Has a grandiose sense of self-importance (e.g., exaggerates achievements and talents, expects to be recognized as superior without commensurate achievements).
2. Is preoccupied with fantasies of unlimited success, power, brilliance, beauty, or ideal love.
3. Believes that he or she [or they] is "special" and unique and can only be understood by, or should associate with, other special or high-status people (or institutions).
4. Requires excessive admiration.
5. Has a sense of entitlement (i.e., unreasonable expectations of especially favorable treatment or automatic compliance with his or her [their] expectations).
6. Is interpersonally exploitative (i.e., takes advantage of others to achieve his or her [or their] own ends).
7. Lacks empathy: is unwilling to recognize or identify with the feelings and needs of others.
8. Is often envious of others or believes that others are envious of him or her [or them].
9. Shows arrogant, haughty behaviors or attitudes.[21]

NPD, a Western understanding of the extreme form of Buddhist "selfing," does not allow for the cultivation of empathy and compassion necessary to allow oneself to be impacted in interreligious dialogue. Since NPD can be experienced by anyone in any religious tradition, one's personality structure should be self-assessed and assessed by the Clinical Pastoral Educators (those who hire, educate, and supervise chaplain residents and interns) interviewer(s) before committing to interreligious dialogue. Assuming there is no NPD or other personality obstructions to interreligious dialogue, there are several ways interreligious dialogue, according to Ingram, can be conducted.

Ingram, drawing on Process Theology and the Natural Sciences, identifies four Buddhist-Christian dialogue processes, including Conceptual Dialogue, Buddhist-Christian Interior Dialogue, Buddhist-Christian Socially Engaged Dialogue, and Conceptual Dialogue with the Natural Sciences. Conceptual Dialogue is when dialogue partners limit their communications to the realm of concepts, discussing whether there is a concept of heaven in Buddhism, for example, or discussing why Christians believe they can live forever, as another example. Buddhist-Christian Interior Dialogue comes as the result of dialogue partners sharing their experiences of contemplation, prayer, and meditation. Buddhist-Christian Socially Engaged Dialogue has to do with matters of justice, peace making, and action. Conceptual Dialogue with the Natural Sciences is a way of knowing whether or not concepts are in accord with nature.

Understanding each process, though none of the processes are directly related to spiritual care in a hospital setting, can contribute to the formulation of a more specific process that supports the expansion of the field of compassionate spiritual care specifically for transgender people. Regarding Conceptual Dialogue, Ingram says,

> The focus of Conceptual Dialogue is doctrinal, theological, and philosophical. It concerns a religious tradition's collective self-understanding and worldview. In Conceptual Dialogue, Buddhists and Christians compare theological and philosophical formulations on such questions as ultimate reality, human nature, suffering and evil, the role of Jesus in Christian faith, the role of the Buddha in Buddhist practice, and what Christians and Buddhists can conceptually learn from one another.[22]

It should be noted here that no matter the concepts under investigation, a Buddhist's ethical duty is to know the concept and detach from it. Nhat Hanh states,

> Life is so precious, too precious to lose just because of these notions and concepts. ... Concepts like "nirvana," "Buddha," "Pure Land," "Kingdom of God," and "Jesus" are just concepts; we have to be very careful. We should not start a war and destroy people because of our concepts.[23]

Certain contexts can support Conceptual Dialogue, like courses and intentional dialogue groups, where time is permitted for the unfolding of doctrine, theology, and philosophy from at least two distinct traditions. The more diverse the traditions, the greater the chances for one to be able to articulate one's own theology and engage others with different theologies.[24] Chaplains-in-training, as well as those who are already on the job, typically do not have the luxury of time. Despite the busy nature of many hospital settings, it would be wise to make time for Buddhist-Christian Spiritual Care Dialogue related to transgender patients. Christian and Buddhist chaplains could begin their dialogues with religious anthropologies, asking questions like, What is a person? Can a person experience illness? Pain? Can a person experience healing? A cure? What is sex? What is gender? What about the body is "sacred," as in, not to be changed? What about a person is permanent? Is a transgender person a "person?" Is a cisgender person a "person?" In short, what about Christianity tells you this being is a person? What about Buddhism tells you this being is a person? How does this square with the Buddhist concepts of no self or nonself?

In addition to Process Theology and Natural Science, Ingram also references theologians Karth Barth, Paul Tillich, Jurgen Moltmann, Karl Rahner, John B. Cobb, Jr., John B. Keenan, Winston L. King, Hans Kung, Seiichi Yagi, Masaaki Honda, Lynn de Silva, and Bihikkhu Buddadasa regarding how to engage in Buddhist-Christian dialogue. This kind of Conceptual Dialogue is purely academic. One can fully engage in Conceptual Dialogue and not become more skilled in giving spiritual care to transgender people, so Conceptual Dialogue alone may stay in the realm of concepts.

Still, on the question of what is a person, Ingram advances the argument that the natural sciences must be brought into dialogue with religious and theological concepts because,

> The natural sciences provide a continual stream of remarkable insights into the nature of physical reality across a wide range of domains. In the process, the natural sciences inspire wonder and, for most scientists and many faithful participants throughout the world's religious traditions, great reverence.[25]

Ingram is aware of how frightening this prospect is for some Christians, especially those who believe in the concept of "intelligent design":

> Most nineteenth-century biologists accepted Darwin's theory, although some, like Louis Agassiz, challenged it by arguing that highly complex

individual organs (like the human eye) and ecologically sensitive species (like bees and flowers) cannot evolve through the sort of minute random steps described by Darwin. To survive, Agassiz argued, each modification must be beneficial. But complex organs and organic relationships only work as a whole. They cannot develop in steps. So he proposed that complex organisms reflect intelligent design, and thus, testify to both the existence and reality of God.[26]

It is this concept and its impulse that contributes to physical, verbal, and emotional aggression as well as the medical neglect of some transgender patients. Intelligent Design Christian chaplains, in a trialogue with natural science and Nhat Hanh's Buddhist teachings, might ask the question, "If the transgender being is a person engaged in intentionally and actively destroying God's intelligent design, how can I be compassionate toward them?" A Buddhist chaplain might ask a Christian chaplain who is an adherent of Intelligent Design, "How can I come to understand gender as something more than a mental construct, something of real importance?" They all may ponder why both sexes have testosterone and estrogen and that hormonal levels change over time. These questions are not meant to be prescribed, but are offered as examples of how to think about natural science and religion together, while keeping in mind the fact that there is a person, or people, in our midst in need of immediate attention.

As a pastoral counselor, I would add here that all of the dialogues need to include psychology, in particular, an understanding Gender Dysphoria (GD).

Gender dysphoria involves a conflict between a person's physical or assigned gender and the gender with which he/she/they identify. People with gender dysphoria *may* be very uncomfortable with the gender they were assigned, sometimes described as being uncomfortable with their body (particularly developments during puberty) or being uncomfortable with the expected roles of their assigned gender.

People with gender dysphoria *may* often experience significant distress and/or problems functioning associated with this conflict between the way they feel and think of themselves (referred to as experienced or expressed gender) and their physical or assigned gender.

The gender conflict affects people in *different ways*. It *can* change the way a person wants to express their gender and *can* influence behavior, dress and self-image. Some people *may* cross-dress, some *may* want to socially transition, others *may* want to medically transition with sex-change surgery and/or hormone treatment. Socially transitioning primarily involves transitioning into the affirmed gender's pronouns and bathrooms [all italics mine].[27]

In this definition are the words "may," "different ways," and "can." It is important to note that the definition of GD is fluid, yet the Trump-Pence administration's military ban on transgender recruits presumes all transgender recruits experience GD and all experience GD in the same way. Chaplains would do very well by transgender patients to avoid totalizing patients in this way.

I add the GD definition not to suggest that one has to agree with it, but to state that chaplains need to understand how psychiatrists view this phenomenon so that a chaplain's spiritual care interventions support the patient's peace of mind and peace of body while they are in the hospital for any reason.

Another Buddhist-Christian dialogue process is Buddhist-Christian Socially Engaged Dialogue. Ingram says,

> Socially engaged Buddhists are uncompromising in the practice of nonviolence, and for Christians this has raised questions about justice. Justice is a central theological category in Christian social activist traditions, but the notion of justice has not played an equivalent role in Buddhism. Christian tradition gives priority to loving engagement with the world as the foundation of establishing justice. So for Christians, the question is to what extent is nonviolent compassion toward all sentient beings, even to aggressors doing harm to whole communities of persons, itself an occasion for injustice?[28]

Buddhist chaplains might ask, "If you say God is love, that Jesus is love, and you commit acts of violence against others, even to save others, is that justifiable?" A Christian chaplain might ask, "How is it compassionate to be a witness to someone else's harm when you could have intervened, but chose not to?" A Buddhist chaplain might ask, "Here we have a transgender patient living in a society that is dangerous. What is your role in advocating for safety for them?" The Christian chaplain might ask, "How can I advocate for those I do not love?" Again, these questions are meant to be examples, not prescriptions. Chaplains of different religions (and no religions) work together to meet the needs of those in their care. In order to offer the most appropriate care possible, they need to talk to one another, know one another, become conversant in other "religion languages," and be able to call on their colleagues when they think they are unable, in the moment, to serve a patient. Chaplains are expected to be empathetic, and of vital importance, be curious about another's belief system.

Buddhist-Christian Interior Dialogue is the communication that comes after participants have contemplated, meditated, or prayed for a considerable amount of time, in silence. Nhat Hanh says,

> I have noticed that Christians and Buddhists who have lived deeply their contemplative lives always come to express themselves in more non-dualistic, nondogmatic ways. Christian mystics and Zen masters never sound speculative or intellectual. Their speculative minds have given way to a non-discursive spirit. Because they have learned not to get caught in notions or representations, they do not speak as though they alone hold the truth, and they do not think that those in other traditions are going the wrong way.[29]

Dialogue partners share what they experience. Ingram writes,

> Buddhist doctrines guide the practice of meditation in all schools of Buddhism. The purpose of Buddhist meditation is to purify the mind of mental distortions caused by clinging to permanence so that one can apprehend the "Emptiness" (*sunyata*) of things and events and thereby not cling to delusions, particularly the delusion of permanent selfhood. Accomplishing this requires a powerfully-concentrated mind. While there exists a plurality of meditative disciplines, five common assumptions guide Buddhist practice traditions, including

> 1. Since the development of mindfulness requires the avoidance of negative activities … ethics is the foundation.
> 2. Meditation can be practiced by concentrating on just one object.
> 3. Meditation can be analytical … through which the reasons and supporting attitudes and emotions … can be apprehended and replaced by non-egoistic emotions.
> 4. Meditation may also be a reflection on the various levels of a spiritual path.
> 5. Meditation may involve visualization techniques, chanting mantras, or simply focusing on one's breathing or a *koan*.[30]

About Christian contemplation, Ingram states, "The goal of Christian contemplative practices of centering prayer and *lectio divina* ('divine reading') is experiential confirmation of the truth of Christian teachings about God as incarnated in the life, death, and resurrection of the historical Jesus."[31] What questions might arise from Buddhist-Christian Interior Dialogue as Ingram identifies these practices?

A Buddhist chaplain might ask a Christian chaplain, "How does your contemplative practice help you connect with Jesus?" And, "Did your connection with Jesus help you connect with _____, the transgender patient?" The Christian chaplain might ask the Buddhist chaplain, "Do you ever use _____'s (the transgender patient) image as an object of meditation? If so, how does that impact how you relate to _____?" Authentic questions will arise as appropriate and the dialogue can proceed from the contemplation, meditation, and development of intrapsychic material.

Somewhere between Buddhist-Christian Conceptual, Socially Engaged, Natural Science, and Interior dialogue is the question of the purpose of the Lord's Prayer, prayed in countless Christian communities and homes throughout the world. It reads,

> Our Father who art in heaven,
> Hallowed be thy name.
> Thy kingdom come.
> Thy will be done
> on earth as it is in heaven.
> Give us this day our daily bread,
> and forgive us our trespasses,
> as we forgive those who trespass against us,
> and lead us not into temptation,
> but deliver us from evil.
> For thine is the kingdom,
> and the power, and the glory,
> for ever and ever
> Amen.

For Buddhists like Nhat Hanh (those who believe the heavenly realm is here but unactualized) in dialogue with Christians refusing to provide appropriate spiritual care for transgender patients, I would begin the dialogue by asking, "What does it mean to you when you pray 'Thy kingdom come, thy will be done, on earth as it is in heaven?'" With this question alone, a dialogue on the concepts of "thy," "kingdom," and "heaven" can begin. The word "earth" can lead into a Natural Science dialogue. "Will be done" can ignite a dialogue on social engagement. The entire prayer itself can lead to a dialogue that is Interior focused. Christians might ask Buddhists, who believe heaven is on earth in the here and now, "What does it feel like? How do you achieve it? What are the hindrances to living a heavenly life now?"

In addition to Ingram's four processes of interreligious dialogue, including Conceptual, Natural Science, Socially Engaged, and Interior, I have added Law, Government, Psychology, and Religious Anthropology. Christians and Buddhists engaged in interreligious dialogue related to the spiritual care of transgender people must also include topics like law and politics in their conversations. For example, regarding the Restoration of Religious Freedom Act (a subject I discuss in Chap. 4) and other laws promulgated for protecting one's religious freedom to discriminate against others, interreligious dialogue partners could discuss the following questions:

1. How do you determine which US citizens should have the religious freedom to discriminate against others?
2. Are you willing to advocate for overturning the equal protection clause of the Fourteenth Amendment?
3. Are you willing to support RFRA at the risk of impoverishing other citizens?
4. If yes, what is your moral obligation to support those you've helped impoverish?
5. What if pure Christianity is determined, in part, on the basis of whether one observes the Sabbath? In America as it is today, nearly 100,000,000 or 29 percent of Americans work on the weekends. Does working on the weekend make one an impure Christian worthy of being discriminated against in the workplace by Sabbath-observing Christians?
6. Should Christians be discriminated against by non-Christians?
7. What are the actual religious practices in your religion that dictate your negative behavior toward transgender citizens?
8. How do you feel about your own sexuality?
9. Keeping Judith Butler in mind, "What are your thoughts on cohabitation?"

According to Winnifred Fallers Sullivan, the chaplain's "religion" or "ministry of presence" is universalist, as in, non-proselytizing. But she asks if this religion of presence is "a conformist kind of religion that accepts law enforcement's categorization of people as law abiders or lawbreakers, or is it a place of resistance to the modern state, sometimes standing with the scofflaw and his Journey?"[32] It could be that the "religion of presence" is conformist for some, as it has been for some CPE interns and residents who need to put their beliefs and practices aside for several weeks or months as they learn the art of spiritual care. For others, the "religion of presence" may be resistance to the modern state and ancient religion. There is at least one more alternative that presence isn't akin to a new kind of religion, but a posture toward the promotion of a civilized society. As it relates to the chaplain's role as a government actor, and as a force for modern state resistance, Buddhist and Christian dialogue partners Nhat Hanh and Catholic priest Daniel Berrigan provide rich examples.

Nhat Hanh and Daniel Berrigan, a Catholic priest, engaged in Interreligious Dialogue on Government in this way:

Berrigan: [engaging in Buddhist-Christian Socially Engaged Dialogue on Government] One has to keep reminding oneself and other people that an exalted contempt for human life lies in the basis of democracy and that one had better think of the unprotected and innocent, and be prepared for bad news when the leaders meet.[33]

Nhat Hanh: These governments always say that for their actions to be effective they must be kept secret. Somewhere their democratic claim goes wrong; it is no longer clear what kind of democracy they dream of.[34]

Berrigan: I think one important aspect of this is the supposition that a well-informed public can change things. "Well-informed" usually involves one or another cliché about the role of the media—the press and television... Because the people can very easily, as in the United States, be lulled into a belief in "free press" and "free television."[35]

Nhat Hanh: So even when there is "free press," a great problem remains.

Berrigan: [engaging in Buddhist-Christian Interior Dialogue] So, the question of selecting, meditating, having some interior life of one's own in the midst of all this, becomes quite important. Especially in such times as these, to have a modest estimation of one's own life—that's a very important form of sanity.[36]

Nhat Hanh: In a situation where fear and hatred and anger prevail, we must still work effectively and we need, very much, the clarity to see, to be serene, to be ourselves first. And then, being so, we can reassure a few friends who are closer to us and can begin to think of something to do.[37]

Berrigan: [This is not engaging the Natural Sciences, but Psychology and arguably touching on Conceptual Dialogue regarding the nature of idolatry] I think fear does two amazing things; maybe they are just aspects of one thing. First, it creates the impression that a person is facing a god, usually a god of war or god of violence; fear makes the adversary look superhuman. Secondly, it creates a new psyche in one's self—a very disrupted, distracted, terrorized person, the opposite of a stable, self-aware person. Two aspects, one fear. If one's soul is so enslaved as to bow to the god, one is already destroyed.[38]

Berrigan and Nhat Hanh engaged in Interreligious Dialogue on Government. They talked about the risks of priests (arguably any religious or spiritual leader) becoming elected officials because of the risks of losing their moral compass and pastoral authority because of the compromises they must make to keep their political jobs as they return favors for votes. Chaplains, even as "secular priests" who work in governmental facilities, such as governmentally funded health care institutions, face similar risks of moral injuries when they do not engage in Interreligious Dialogue about Government and their roles as government agents. One way chaplains can avoid losing their moral compass and maintain their pastoral authority is by voicing their opinions in the public sphere about politicians promulgating religious freedom laws to discriminate against minority populations.

In a political era where hospitals (and other health care organizations) have become ground zero for the religious freedom to discriminate against transgender people, should health care employees, through compassion, become part of a political resistance to discriminating against patients in their care? Berrigan and Nhat Hanh, in their Socially Engaged Dialogue, did not discuss hospital contexts or trans people, but discussed the role of chaplains in the prison (governmental institutions) context, and they came to an agreement that prison chaplains should not have the power to imprison others while also attempting to provide them spiritual care. Berrigan said:

> The problem of how you minister to prisoners remains. It's not solved by saying that you come and go with a bunch of keys. *A way must be found to prevent chaplains from taking the salary of the state and standing in the same relationship to prisoners as the guards. Such a chaplain is looking for the same benefits* [my emphasis]; he goes up the ladder the way the guards do in salary and in rank, and he retires with a pension, just as they do. This can't help but affect his relationship to the prisoners. In fact, Philip [Daniel's brother] and I have never met a prison chaplain whom we could respect. Not one.[39]

Chaplains, especially cisgender chaplains in health care contexts caring for transgender patients, can ask ourselves similar questions about our cisgender privileges vis-à-vis the health care institutions we are admitted. Why does being cisgender permit us to be cared for? We can ask ourselves in what way or ways do we partner with institutions to diminish the trans patients we serve and ask ourselves if we are doling out "cheap grace" to those patients rather than spiritual care of little transformative value? In other words, have cisgender chaplains become complicit with health care systems of trans oppression if we are not resisting discriminatory policies and laws?

In addition to chaplains in the prison context, Nhat Hanh and Berrigan talk about communities of resistance.

Berrigan: I think the word *resistance* [my emphasis] became very important around 1967 in the States. People were saying that it was necessary to take a step beyond protest. We could no longer look upon our style of life as merely being an occasion for this or that action. People had to begin thinking much more seriously and deeply about a long-term struggle in which they would stand up more visibly and perhaps with more risk. ... One person refusing induction or going on trial or leaving the university would have no impact. Now there must be a community behind him.[40]

Nhat Hanh: I think that's a very meaningful term. And *resistance* [my emphasis], at root, I think, must mean more than resistance against war. It is a resistance against all kinds of things that are like war. Because living in modern society, one feels that

> he cannot easily retain integrity, wholeness. One is robbed
> permanently of humanness, the capacity of being oneself. ...
> So perhaps, first of all, resistance means you lose yourself.
> So perhaps, first of all, resistance means opposition to being
> invaded, occupied, assaulted, and destroyed by the system.
> The purpose of resistance, here, is to seek the healing of
> yourself in order to be able to see clearly.[41]

Buddhist and Christian chaplains, through Interreligious Dialogue on
Government, can learn from each other about their religious identities
and obligations to resist oppression as they provide spiritual care to
transgender patients in government-funded health care institutions. Based
on my research, chaplains, pastoral counselors, and chaplain educators are
not collectively resisting policies and laws *as religious and spiritual
professionals*, that promote hatred and neglect of trans people.

Throughout Nhat Hanh's writings, he reflects a conceptual gender
fluidity as it relates to transcending bodily forms in the mystical Avatamsaka
world. This mystical world, for Nhat Hahn, is God/Holy Spirit itself,
expressed in material form in our unrealized consciousness.

> In the phenomenal world, we see that there is birth and death. There is
> coming and going, being and non-being. But in nirvana, which is the
> ground of being equivalent to God, there is no birth, no death, no coming,
> no going, no being, no non-being. All these concepts must be transcended.[42]

In nirvana, the dualistic "concepts" of male or female and the "concept"
transgender are transcended. It is likely Paul, Jesus's apostle, would have
agreed. In The Letter of Paul to the Galatians, he says,

> For you are all sons of God through faith in Christ Jesus. For as many of you
> as were baptized into Christ have put on Christ. There is neither Jew nor
> Greek, there is neither slave nor free, there is neither male nor female; for
> you are all one in Christ Jesus. And if you are Christ's then you are Abraham's
> seed, and heirs according to the promise.[43]

In Paul's letter to Colossians, he says,

> But now you yourselves are to put off all these: anger, wrath, malice, blas-
> phemy, filthy language out of your mouth. Do not lie to one another, since
> you have put off the old man with his deeds, and have put on the new man

who is renewed in knowledge according to the image of Him who created him, where there is neither Greek nor Jew, circumcised nor uncircumcised, barbarian, Scythian, slave nor free, but Christ is all and in all.[44]

Nhat Hanh and Paul, like the Buddha and Jesus, are mystical kinfolk of non-dualistic, unifying consciousness that fades away, lessens in importance, loses its power to separate and discriminate, loses its hierarchal meanings, yet brings spirit-world beings together as one. Christian and Buddhist chaplains in dialogue about caring for transgender patients can expand the field of compassionate care by engaging in dialogue about their respective unifying spiritual practices that promote nondiscrimination and support one another in those practices while staying within their religious homes, radically co-inhabiting the clinical space of the pluralistic hospital setting. A true cohabitation of constructive interreligious dialogue that incorporates wisdom, compassion, constitutional vigilance, advocacy, activism, care, and analysis will likely shock a health care system out of fear of, hatred toward, ignorance about, and neglect of caring for transgender patients into a system striving to be hospitable toward all.

Recalling the lawyer who asked Jesus "Who is my neighbor?" it is important to know that the government has a compelling interest in helping its citizens prevent disease (Centers for Disease Control), rehabilitate veterans of war (Veteran's Administration and Hospitals), be healthy (governmental hospitals), and reduce medical costs (Medicaid and Medicare). These compelling governmental interests can be balanced with protecting religious freedom in responsible ways, and chaplains are perfectly positioned to lead the way in demonstrating how these governmental interests may be balanced.

Notes

1. Winnifred Fallers Sullivan, *A Ministry of Presence: Chaplaincy, Spiritual Care, and the Law* (Chicago: The University of Chicago Press, 2014), 64.
2. Luke 10:25–37. Unless otherwise noted, all scriptural passages are from the Thompson Chain-Reference Study Bible, New King James Version, compiled and edited by Frank Charles Thompson, published by B.B. Kirkbridge Bible Co., Inc., Indianapolis, IN.
3. Trump Rolls Back Transgender Bathroom Guidelines For Schools. http://fortune.com/2017/02/22/trump-lgbt-transgender-bathroom-guidelines/ (Accessed September 12, 2018).

4. President Donald J. Trump Proclaims January 16, 2018, as Religious Freedom Day. https://www.whitehouse.gov/presidential-actions/president-donald-j-trump-proclaims-january-16-2018-religious-freedom-day/ (Accessed September 3, 2018).

5. "This Is Not America," from *The Falcon and the Snowman* soundtrack, written by Bowie, Pat Metheny, and Lyle Mays. https://en.wikipedia.org/wiki/This_Is_Not_America (1985) (Accessed September 21, 2018).

6. The Discrimination Administration, https://transequality.org/the-discrimination-administration (Accessed September 12, 2018).

7. Erica L. Green, Katie Benner and Robert Pear, 'Transgender' Could be Defined Out of Existence Under Trump Administration, https://www.nytimes.com/2018/10/21/us/politics/transgender-trump-administration-sex-definition.html (Accessed January 9, 2019).

8. Lawarence Hurley, "U.S. court rules for Trump on transgender military limits," https://www.reuters.com/article/us-usa-court-transgender/us-court-rules-for-trump-on-transgender-military-limits-idUSKCN1OY1BI (Accessed January 9, 2019).

9. https://www.etymonline.com/word/hospital (accessed August 27, 2018).

10. Sullivan, 86.

11. Winnifred Fallers Sullivan, *A Ministry of Presence: Chaplaincy, Spiritual Care, and the Law* (Chicago: The University of Chicago Press, 2014), 3.

12. Ibid., 38. Though Sullivan is quoting from Veteran Affairs documents, it is the case in many hospitals and hospices that chaplains are part of the health care team that includes social workers, nurses, doctors, and others.

13. Ibid., 50.

14. Finnegan, Joanne, "As complaints trickle in, protecting workers' religious rights could cost health industry upward of $300M in First Year, FierceHealth, https://www.fiercehealthcare.com/practices/protecting-workers-religious-rights-cost-healthcare-300m-donald-trump-hhs-roger-severino, February 6, 2018, (Accessed January 12, 2019).

15. Ibid., 17.

16. Minority Quotes https://www.brainyquote.com/topics/minority (Accessed September 12, 2018).

17. Mendieta and Vanantwerpen, eds., *The Power of Religion in the Public Sphere*, New York, Columbia Press, 2011, 118.

18. Ibid., 76.

19. Nhat Hanh, *Living Buddha, Living Christ*, Riverhead Books, 1995, 2007, 196.

20. Nhat Hanh, *Living Buddha, Living Christ*, Riverhead Books, 1995, 2007, 9.

21. American Psychiatric Association, *Desk Reference to the Diagnostic Criteria from DSM-5*, American Psychiatric, Publishing, Washington, DC (2013), 327.
22. Ingram, 29.
23. Nhat Hanh, *Going Home: Jesus and Buddha As Brothers*, Riverhead Books, 1999, 82.
24. Liam Muggleton Robins, CPE educator, personal communication, February 17, 2019.
25. Paul O. Ingram, *The Process of Buddhist-Christian Dialogue*, 2009, 54.
26. Ibid., 66.
27. "What is Gender Dsyphoria" https://www.psychiatry.org/patients-families/gender-dysphoria/what-is-gender-dysphoria (Accessed October 29, 2018).
28. Ibid., 84.
29. Nhat Hanh, *Living Buddha, Living Christ*, Riverhead Books, 1995, 2007, 179–180.
30. Ibid., 112.
31. Ibid.
32. Sullivan, xvi.
33. Thich Nhat Hanh and Daniel Berrigan, *The Raft is Not the Shore: Conversations Toward a Buddhist-Christian Awareness*, Maryknoll, New York, Orbis, 2001, 73.
34. Ibid.
35. Ibid., 74.
36. Ibid., 75.
37. Ibid., 79.
38. Ibid., 80.
39. Ibid., 55–57.
40. Ibid., 128.
41. Ibid., 129.
42. Nhat Hanh, *Going Home: Buddha and Jesus As Brothers* (1997), 10.
43. Galatians 3:26–29, *The Thompson Chain-Reference Study* Bible, B.B. Kirkbridge Bible Co., Inc. Indianapolis, IN, 1997, 1512.
44. Colossians 3:8–11, *The Thompson Chain-Reference Study* Bible, B.B. Kirkbridge Bible Co., Inc. Indianapolis, IN, 1997, 1530.

CHAPTER 2

Spiritual Care and Political Involvement, Womanist Public Theology, and Boston Medical Center

Abstract Chaplains, pastoral counselors, and Clinical Pastoral Education (CPE) educators and supervisors are surveyed regarding their knowledge about religious freedom to discriminate laws, their advocacy for the oppressed, and their curricula regarding religious freedom law. The chaplain at Boston Medical Center (BMC) is interviewed about how she educates CPE interns about spiritual care for transgender patients, and BMC's Medical Director for the Center for Transgender Medicine and Surgery is interviewed about her work with transgender patients, as well as her work with chaplaincy. Theologically educated political scientist, professor, and television host Melissa Harris-Perry's work is explicated as womanist public practical theology.

Keywords Boston Medical Center • Chaplain • Clinical Pastoral Education • Melissa Harris-Perry • Pastoral Counselor

Earlier this week I was consulted to see a transgender patient preparing for surgery. She was very anxious about the surgery because she had been attacked at another hospital. Her faith was a resource for her, as was her church community. I listened to her and we prayed before surgery. I saw her the next day and we had a long conversation about her life, faith, and longing to become the person God wants her to be. Through her transition and traumatic experiences associated with transitioning,

© The Author(s) 2020
P. A. Yetunde, *Buddhist-Christian Dialogue, U.S. Law, and Womanist Theology for Transgender Spiritual Care,*
https://doi.org/10.1007/978-3-030-42560-9_2

> *she maintains incredible integrity and courage, with support from her*
> *faith community and family.*
> *(Anonymous source, personal communication, January 21, 2019)*

Chaplain educators, chaplains, and pastoral counselors are professionally trained Good Samaritans, culturally speaking, and need a motivating ethic to inspire their engagement in Interreligious Dialogue on Government and Law. The religious freedom rhetoric of the Trump-Pence administration, as well as the creation of the Department of Health and Human Services Office for Civil Rights Conscience and Religious Freedom Division (CRFD), creates a potentially toxic and dangerous hospital environment for transgender patients. Although experienced spiritual caregivers have dedicated years of their lives to learning about the ways people suffer and heal, are they willing now to dedicate the next years to creating radically inclusive cohabitable safe spaces for all patients through public advocacy?

WOMANIST-INSPIRED PUBLIC THEOLOGY, RELIGIOUS FREEDOM LAW LITERACY, AND CHAPLAINS CREATING SAFE SPACES

Chaplains, pastoral counselors, and chaplain educators do not organize well by professions to publicly advocate for responsible religious freedom practices that would protect trans people from discrimination in health care settings. Is it possible we aren't as knowledgeable about religious freedom laws and policies as we think we are? Are we obligated, as health care professions and healers, to attempt to prevent harmful practices?

These questions come out of my own understanding of the roots of novelist, poet, and activist Alice Walker womanism. Walker defines a womanist as,

A woman who loves other women, sexually and/or nonsexually. Appreciates and prefers women's culture, women's emotional flexibility (values tears as natural counterbalance of laughter), and women's *strength*. Sometimes loves individual men, sexually and/or nonsexually. Committed to survival and wholeness of entire people, male *and* female. (This was written in 1983, pre-trans competency era.) Not a separatist, except periodically, for health. Traditionally universalist, as in "Mama, why are we brown, pink, and yellow, and our cousins are white, beige, and black?" Answer: "Well, you know the colored race is just like a flower garden, with every color flower represented." *Traditionally capable*, as in "Mama, I'm walking to Canada and I'm taking you and a bunch of other slaves with me." Reply: "It wouldn't be the first time."[1]

This description helped usher womanist Christian theology into a discipline of scholarship among African-American women theologians. My personal definition of womanism, informed by Walker's 1979 short story *Coming Apart* (where the word "womanist" first appears), is as follows:

> Womanism is the willingness on the part of women of all sexualities to seek out wisdom from African-American lesbians on *how to create safe spaces* for themselves, in the *midst of threats* to their emotional, mental, physical, and spiritual health, and *take the risk* of sharing that wisdom with their *oppressor(s) in a way that does not harm* the oppressor(s), with the intention to help the oppressor(s) awaken from ignorance and violence, and *to be advocates for African-American lesbians in the African-American community.*[2]

Rather than focus on the African-American women-exclusive nature of my definition, I want to focus on creating safe spaces and echoing Walker's commitment to survival and wholeness of entire groups of people. Do spiritual caregivers live out the universalist attitude of survival and wholeness of entire groups of people by creating safe spaces where there is no safety?

On January 12, 2017, anticipating that the Trump-Pence administration would continue its charge to advance the religious freedom to discriminate, I crafted and distributed two online surveys, one for chaplains and one for pastoral counselors, to determine their level of awareness of religious freedom laws. Forty-three chaplains and 34 pastoral counselors responded. The surveys were limited to the South, where I lived at the time, including Alabama, Florida, Georgia, Mississippi, North Carolina, South Carolina, and Tennessee. In the Religious Freedom for Chaplains survey, I asked the following questions:

1. Is being a chaplain part of your professional identity?
2. Where do you live?
3. Are you board certified?
4. Are you familiar with the federal Religious Freedom Restoration Act of 1993?

5. Are you familiar with your state's religious freedom law, if any?
6. Do you believe you should have the right to refuse spiritual care on religious grounds?
7. In what context do you offer professional spiritual care?
8. Have you provided expert advice to lawmakers drafting your state's religious freedom law?
9. Have you lobbied for or against your state's religious freedom laws?
10. Please state up to three questions you think should be on the final survey?
11. Do you believe religious freedom laws that allow discrimination against groups of people can negatively impact a chaplain's compassion or empathy?
12. Have you ever participated in a survey about federal or state religious freedom laws?

In the Pastoral Counselors Religious Freedom Pre-survey I asked:

1. Is "pastoral counseling" part of your professional identity? ("Pastoral counseling" is a term that may be synonymous with or akin to pastoral psychotherapy, spiritual direction, spiritual psychotherapy, spiritually aware counseling, etc.)
2. Where do you live?
3. Are you a member of the Southeast Region of the American Association of Pastoral Counselors?
4. Are you familiar with the federal Religious Freedom Restoration Act of 1993?
5. Are you familiar with your state's religious freedom law, if any?
6. Have your state's religious freedom laws had an impact on who you provide counseling for?
7. Have you provided expert advice to lawmakers drafting your state's religious freedom law?
8. Have you lobbied for or against your state's religious freedom laws?
9. Please state up to three questions you think should be on the final survey.
10. Do you believe religious freedom laws that allow discrimination against groups of people can negatively impact a pastoral counselor's compassion or empathy?
11. Have you ever participated in a survey about federal or state religious freedom laws?

Regarding the Religious Freedom Restoration Act of 1993 (RFRA), 45 percent of chaplains said they were unfamiliar with RFRA, and 47 percent of pastoral counselors said they were somewhat familiar with RFRA, with 35 percent stating that they were unfamiliar with the legislation. Forty-two percent of chaplains and 44 percent of pastoral counselors said they were unfamiliar with their state's religious freedom law. Sixty-five percent of the chaplain respondents worked in hospital settings; the pastoral counselors did not. None of the chaplains in the study and only one of the surveyed pastoral counselors had provided expert advice to lawmakers drafting religious freedom laws. A disconnect exists between pastoral care professionals in the South and their legislators. Most research participants were not familiar with RFRA or their state religious freedom laws and did not offer their expertise to lawmakers. As it relates to religious freedom laws and their impact on spiritual caregivers, 45 percent of chaplains and 38 percent of pastoral counselors believe these laws can have a negative impact on their ability to be compassionate and empathetic toward targeted groups of people. Twenty-five percent of the chaplains and 12 percent of pastoral counselors did not believe these laws impacted their ability to be compassionate and empathetic toward targeted groups.

Will the belief that these laws could negatively impact the spiritual care profession be enough to propel spiritual and pastoral caregivers to become activists for the free exercise of responsible religious freedom? Will we take our private theologies public? The lack of religious-freedom-law literacy and responsible religious freedom advocacy among spiritual care providers, with a concentration of chaplains in hospitals, poses a potentially dangerous spiritual pit for transgender patients as well as a positive opportunity for education that could lead to a deepening of compassion and advocacy for vulnerable populations.

Regarding the question, "Do you believe you should have the right to refuse spiritual care on religious grounds?", 65 percent of chaplains responded affirmatively. Yet, 97 percent of pastoral counselors said their state's religious freedom laws had not had an impact on whom they provided counseling to. I suspect there is a difference in the spiritual and vocational formation of chaplains and pastoral counselors in that the spiritual and vocational formation of chaplains is usually a prerequisite to becoming a pastoral counselor. In doctoral-level pastoral counselor education, one who has been a chaplain is supervised and educated in psychotherapy and supervised in the clinical practices of spiritually integrated psychotherapy. Regarding the question, "Do you believe religious freedom laws that allow discrimination against groups of people can negatively impact a pastoral counselor's compassion or empathy?", 50 percent of pastoral counselors answered "Maybe," 12 percent answered "No," and 38 percent answered "Yes." But the spiritual caregivers in these surveys did not involve themselves in the politics of religious freedom. Ninety-seven percent of pastoral counselors and all of the chaplains said they had never provided expert advice to lawmakers drafting their states' religious freedom laws.

If these surveys are an indication of the level of awareness of laws and legislative processes and the level of involvement in offering expertise to lawmakers among spiritual care professionals, the professions should examine the perils to them and those they serve and decide whether or not becoming politically involved is a part of what it means to be a spiritual care professional. What does it mean that those who profess love, compassion, empathy, and care for the least of these allow systems of injustice and oppression to morph, grow, and impact vulnerable populations, especially transgender people? What does it say about spiritual and pastoral care professionals that we are largely removed from educating lawmakers about our work? Do we deserve the trust given to us by patients and clients who are targeted in the midst of our silence?

In a subsequent study launched on August 21, 2018, while I was a post-doctoral research fellow at Harvard Divinity School, I sent a survey to chaplain educators working in hospitals throughout the United States. The survey questions included:

1. Are you working as a chaplain supervisor or educator in a hospital?
2. How many years have you worked as a chaplain supervisor or educator in a hospital?
3. What kind of hospital do you work in?
4. What best defines your religious or nonreligious identity(ies)?
5. Where in the U.S. is your hospital located?
6. Are you aware of the rights in the First Amendment of the U.S. Constitution?
7. Do you educate chaplain interns and residents about the First Amendment?
8. Do you educate residents and interns about the Fourteenth Amendment's equal protection clause?
9. If you educate interns and residents about the U.S. Constitution, what resources do you use?

10. Are you aware of the rights in the Religious Freedom Restoration Act of 1993?
11. Do you educate chaplain interns and residents about the Religious Freedom Restoration Act of 1993?
12. Are you aware of the U.S. Department of Health and Human Services (HHS) Office for Civil Rights and its mandate of protecting religious freedom for health care workers?
13. Do you educate chaplain interns and residents about the HHS religious freedom exemption?
14. Has a chaplaincy intern or resident asked for a HHS religious freedom exemption?
15. Have you asked for a HHS religious freedom exemption?
16. Do you anticipate asking for a HHS religious freedom exemption for yourself?
17. If you anticipate asking for a HHS religious freedom exemption for yourself, describe the kind of person you would withhold giving spiritual care to?
18. As it relates to chaplain educators and supervisors helping interns and residents cultivate compassion for those who are not a part of their religious group, what is most important?
19. How do you cultivate compassion for those outside your religious group?
20. Who are the people your religion defines as "less than" or unworthy of receiving compassion from someone in your religious tradition?
21. What professional chaplaincy organization(s) are you a part of?
22. How do you help interns and residents resolve conflicts between their religion, the U.S. Constitution, HHS Civil Rights, and chaplaincy professional code of ethics related to nondiscrimination?

The results indicate a discrepancy between what chaplain educators know about religious freedom laws and what they teach to chaplains-in-training.

Thirty-nine people completed the survey; five of them said they were not chaplain educators in hospital settings. Fifty-three percent worked in public hospitals; 24 percent worked in private, not-religion-based hospitals; and nearly 22 percent worked in religion-based hospitals. Fifty-nine percent identified as Christian-Protestant, and 17 percent identified as Christian-Catholic.[3] Respondents were from 17 states, spanning across the United States; 32 percent were from Minnesota.[4]

All of the chaplain educators claimed they were aware of the rights in the First Amendment, but 69 percent did not educate their interns and residents about the First Amendment. A higher percentage, 75 percent, did not educate their students about the Fourteenth Amendment. Sixty-five percent were aware of the rights in the Religious Freedom Restoration Act of 1993, but 78 percent of chaplain educators did not teach their interns and students about it. Most educators, 62 percent, were aware of the Health and Human Services Office for Civil Rights and its protection of religious freedom for health care workers, but 72 percent did not educate their students about it. If this survey is an indication of a nationwide trend, most chaplain educators are not talking to their students about religious freedom laws. This gap creates an extraordinary opportunity for interdisciplinary spiritual and vocational formation.

None of the chaplain educators in this survey anticipated asking for a religious exemption from caring for another. Forty-four percent of chaplain educators did not believe their religions excluded people from receiving spiritual care. Given this response, it is reasonable to expect that chaplain educators can teach their students how to become radically accepting of people different from themselves. When asked, "As it relates to chaplain educators and supervisors helping interns and residents cultivate compassion for those who are not a part of their religious group, what is important?", respondents chose the following responses: professional standards of care (21 percent), chaplaincy organization's professional code of ethics (20 percent), hospital professional expectation (20 percent), their own values (12 percent), the interns' or residents' own religious traditions and practices (8 percent), and the U.S. Constitution (7 percent).[5] Do chaplain educators believe interns' and residents' own religious traditions and practices do not adequately prepare them to offer compassionate care? Why is the U.S. Constitution not deemed an educational tool to help chaplain educators teach about compassion? Chaplain educators use ethical commitments (23 percent), advocacy (21 percent), selfless service (16 percent), prayer (15 percent), and meditation (12 percent) to help their students cultivate compassion for those outside their religious groups.[6] Ethical commitments ranks higher than the religious and spiritual practices of prayer and meditation. Will this remain the case with the Trump-Pence religious freedom political rhetoric and HHS's Conscience and Religious Freedom Division's enforcement mechanism inspiring religious adherence, even above the law? The ability of chaplain educators to advocate for others can be taken beyond the institutional contexts where they serve into community and legislative contexts. There is an opportunity for improving advocacy skills for other extra-clinical contexts.

Influenced by womanist definitions to think about the ethical commitment to creating safe spaces for the survival and wholeness of entire peoples, I have been inspired by journalist Melissa Harris-Perry, an African-American, cisgender, straight, feminist, professor and activist. Harris-Perry is Maya Angelou Presidential Chair at Wake Forest University. She is founding director of the Anna Julia Cooper Center and the faculty director of the Pro Humanitate Institute. From 2012 to 2016, Harris-Perry hosted a television show on MSNBC. Over the course of its time on MSNBC, Harris-Perry's program gained in popularity, especially among Democrats aged 25–54. In February of 2016, Harris-Perry stopped hosting her show, claiming that the network was silencing her. She was fired that March. Since 2010, Harris-Perry has publicly advocated for responsible religious freedom practices.

In 2010, Harris-Perry wrote, "The recent reemergence of conservative, biblical claims renews my sense that we need to cultivate an active, public, prophetic, liberal core that can resist these texts of terror [against LGBTQ people] by arguing for a more comprehensive engagement with the bible."[7] In 2011, in an interview in *Religion Dispatches* about her speech at the Human Rights Campaign Clergy Call, Harris-Perry, citing verses instructing slaves to obey their masters, said, "There are all sorts of things that we've decided we no longer read in the way they were once read. People are still wrestling with Pauline claims about wives submitting themselves to their husbands." She says people who don't live by those verses haven't rejected them because they learned something new about the texts, but because they learned, or came to appreciate, something about the greater whole."[8] Harris-Perry published *Sister Citizen: Shame, Stereotypes, and Black Women in America* that same year. In 2012, Harris-Perry took on the Catholic Church's stance against government-mandated contraception as a religious freedom issue.[9] In 2013 she taught Black Religion and Black Political Thought. The course objective stated, "This course will use a variety of classic and contemporary texts about black political thought as an entry into investigating the connections between black religious ideas and political activism. The class links the work on religion to an intensive introduction to black political thought."[10] In her open letter to then-Governor of Mississippi Phil Bryant, Harris-Perry read in 2014:

And you can already be discriminated against for your sexual orientation in Mississippi. You can be fired or not hired just for being gay. You can be denied housing. So, governor, what you did was make it even easier than it already was to discriminate against LGBT Mississippians. ...

That's not all the Religious Freedom Restoration Act does. It also adds the words "In God We Trust" to the official state seal, something that was such a legislative priority for you that you made special reference to it in your January State of the State address. ...

"In God We Trust." But that goes both ways, governor. The way God works—at least in the Christian tradition, which you and 84 percent of Mississippians follow—the way God works is *through* his followers. "Feed my sheep," Jesus said. ...

Sincerely,

Melissa[11]

Can Harris-Perry's sustained advocacy for the LGBTQ community be an inspiration to chaplains, pastoral counselors, chaplain educators, and spiritual caregivers who tend toward private acts of healing and advocacy within clinical settings, but who remain virtually silent as it relates to public policy, lobbying, and collective public advocacy for trans people?

Melissa Harris-Perry identifies as a feminist. Alice Walker, in defining womanism, remarked that womanism is to feminism as purple is to lavender. It is a matter of shade. I argue that Harris-Perry, who claims an African-American identity, who has hosted many people of color, including African-Americans, on her show, and who was brave enough to take Dr. Cornell West to task for his criticisms of former President Barack Obama, is deeply shaded toward the purple. In her book *Sister Citizen: Shame, Stereotypes, and Black Women in America*, she says of womanism,

> *Womanism* was the term these black women scholars gave to the work of crafting a fully articulated racialized and gendered theology. *Womanism* was coined as a description of black feminist sensibilities by Alice Walker in her book *In Search of Our Mothers' Gardens*. Walker describes womanism as an intense form of female-centered identification and action most often exhibited among women of color. Womanism lays claim to the intersectional experience of race and gender for women of color. Walker's definition also conveys a sense of the strong black woman.

The sense of the *mythological* strong black woman comes, I argue, from the separation of Walker's 1983 womanist definition from the 1979 short story *Coming Apart*, where she first coined the word "womanist" out of a fictional story about a very vulnerable woman.[12] Womanist also includes "...(values tears as natural counterbalance of laughter), and women's strength."[13]

Womanist pastoral theologian, psychologist, and Christian minister Chanequa Walker-Barnes says of vulnerability,

> Anger is a favored emotion over sadness. In a classic "fight or flight" style, when the StrongBlackWoman cannot avoid or flee vulnerability, she assumes a fighter's stance, preferring the active emotions of anger, irritability, disgust, contempt, and annoyance.
>
> Such fear of vulnerability is likely an inevitable consequence of the burden of strength. In order to reduce vulnerability, StrongBlackWomen often rely excessively upon the defense mechanisms of repression and suppression to deal with negative emotions. Despite their seemingly stoic demeanor in the face of stress, StrongBlackWomen are no more impervious to the difficulties of life than anyone else. That is, they experience fear, sadness, grief, and worry to the same extent as do other people.[14]

The stoicism Walker-Barnes describes can manifest as silence. She says,

> And while "silent" is not often a descriptor attributed to StrongBlackWomen, it aptly describes the process by which African-American women suppress the repressed feelings of vulnerability as they attempt to live up to the myth of strength.[15]

Reflecting on Walker, Harris-Perry, and Walker-Barnes, could it be that chaplains, pastoral counselors, and spiritual caregivers are formed in such a way that they subconsciously take on the qualities of the StrongBlackWoman, regardless of the myriad ways they define themselves, so that they appear impervious to vulnerability in the face of suffering? What explains silence in legislative and political matters? Why don't spiritual care providers act collectively to create safe spaces for transgender patients? Why not engage the Human Rights Campaign (HRC), for example, submitting spiritual care departments to HRC's scrutiny and consultation? Why do chaplain educators like Rev. Dr. Gould (her interview appears in this chapter) of Boston Medical Center find themselves educating several interns at once in busy public hospital settings without administrative help? Is there a myth of the StrongChaplain operative in our contexts? What can spiritual caregivers of all identities learn from black women about the myth of the StrongBlackWoman and the reality of vulnerability?

Harris-Perry is an African-American cisgender, straight woman who has sought wisdom from African-American pro-women women (alive and deceased), including poet Nikki Giovanni, writers Rebecca Walker and Alice Walker, lawyer and minister Pauli Murray, and activist and professor Angela Y. Davis, to name a few. These women have written and/or spoken about how to address chronic vulnerabilities related to racism, sexism, genderism, classism, and mass incarceration. As a television-show host Harris-Perry shared that wisdom with those who would listen, in an intellectual and respectful manner, with the intention of helping people awaken from ignorance and violence. She has been a staunch advocate for LGBTQ people and other marginalized people, in and outside the African-American community. It is our chronic vulnerability, including the ways Christian supremacy and transphobia contribute to that chronic vulnerability, that makes Harris-Perry's black-Christian-feminist-womanist public theology critical. Harris-Perry's public theological methods for being an advocate include scholarship, teaching, public lectures, a television show, acknowledging some Biblical texts as irredeemably oppressive, writing, more comprehensive engagement with the Bible, and elevating "countering texts of liberation."[16] This is how she contributes to the creation of safe spaces for marginalized people.

With my womanist sensibilities, observations of an encroaching oppressive political-religious force against trans people, and findings from surveys of chaplains and pastoral counselors, I decided to complete a case study on Boston Medical Center's (BMC) Clinical Pastoral Education program. BMC is unique in the northeast for its transgender medical care. It received a perfect score from the Human Rights Campaign.[17] Due to its commitment to transgender people and its excellent standard of care, I thought BMC would be a good study in how a hospital CPE program might promote the creation of safe spaces and the cultivation of compassion for transgender people.

Boston Medical Center

Given increases in religious-freedom-to-discriminate enforcement and attacks on transgender people, including transcleansing,[18] I wanted to better discern the quality of care provided to trans patients at BMC's Center for Transgender Medicine and Surgery (CTMS). I looked to the 2018

Human Rights Campaign Health Equality Index (HEI) as a benchmark for high-quality service. BMC's CTMS website is an education in transgender cultural appropriateness, and I have italicized words and phrases I believe are important for pastoral caregivers to use in order to be appropriate spiritual presences for trans hospital patients. The website reads, in part,

> Boston Medical Center provides comprehensive *trans-friendly* services. Our primary care providers support *trans and gender incongruent* individuals from adolescence through adulthood.
>
> BMC offers behavioral health services for people considering gender transition designed to assist in evaluating the choices available and to better cope with the psychological difficulties inherent in such a serious decision. Psychological counseling during hormone treatment is usually supportive in nature and is intended to assist the individual in overcoming societal, family or personal issues inherent in this process. For individuals who do not identify as either male or female, psychological services provide a safe and nonjudgmental environment to explore one's identity and gender related issues.
>
> Boston Medical Center is a leader in hormone treatment for transgender individuals and serves as a referral center for transgender hormone therapy for all adults. Transmen and transwomen can be referred by their primary care providers. Available endocrine services include initial consultations, active monitoring/prescribing/management of hormone regimens, guidance with complex medical concerns, and second opinions about hormone treatment strategies.
>
> BMC provides care and guidance for individuals whose primary care providers are more knowledgeable about transgender care as well as for individuals with less knowledgeable primary care providers. We can support patients and their providers with education as required to enable patients to maintain relationships with providers convenient to them.
>
> How one sounds when they speak with others is crucial to *affirming an identity*. The Center for Voice and Swallowing offers high-quality voice and communication therapy so that a patient's voice and how they present themselves will *match with their preferred expression of identity*.[19]

BMC's CTMS website suggests a trans-friendly practice that offers a variety of experts. There is no mention, however, of the fact that CTMS works closely with the chaplaincy department. Searching the word "chaplaincy" leads here:

> Please ask your nurse if you'd like to have a chaplain or clergy members visit you. Religious services are televised on the hospital's internal channel 6,

which also lists the times of the services, the names of chaplains and their telephone numbers. There are also two Interfaith Chapels available for meditation and prayer.[20]

Combining search terms "Boston Medical Center" and "chaplaincy" leads here:

> The Spiritual Care Department works collaboratively to help patients, family members and staff to address emotional, spiritual and religious needs. We serve as liaisons, connecting members of the healthcare team, patients and families, and—if requested—clergy or other religious leaders in the community.
>
> Our multi-faith team provides *inclusive* spiritual care and can explore how your own sense of faith and spirituality may be a healing, comforting resource to you. We will address your *unique* spiritual journey and support your needs when an ordinary sense of meaning and hope has been disrupted by illness, sudden hospitalization or a life-changing event.
>
> Chaplains value the uniqueness of each person's spiritual path and provide compassionate support to those of *all* religious traditions and those who are unaffiliated but seeking support.

The chaplaincy webpage includes contact information, information on the availability of chaplains and "faith-specific" chaplains, descriptions of services, advice on when it is appropriate to call a chaplain, and advice, support, and encouragement for staff in need of spiritual care.[21]

To develop an understanding of how BMC's CTMS might inspire other hospitals to cultivate compassion for transgender hospital patients, I interviewed Rev. Dr. Jennie R. Gould, chaplain educator and hospital chaplain, and Dr. Jennifer Siegel, medical director for the CTMS. I wanted to learn how they work together to achieve their high rating from the Human Rights Campaign. Given the limits of this text, I will focus on only a few best practices and identify only a few opportunities for additional practices. I began the case study by sharing interview questions with Rev. Dr. Gould via email. Our conversation follows.

How do you describe your role?
Educator, advocate, cultural broker, ethicist, facilitator, support for staff—especially in times of crisis or moral distress—relationship builder/connector with local religious leaders, ritual celebrant. I could go on, but I'll stop here.

Do you educate your students on how to provide compassionate pastoral/spiritual care to transgender patients?
Yes.

If yes, what does "compassionate pastoral/spiritual care" for transgender patients mean to you?
Education on vocabulary that enhances respect and caring for the whole person; cis privilege (within context of understanding dominant power structures and systemic sins); empathy for both the struggle and courage of our trans patients; examining power and control (in partner violence presentation) and scripture passages that support this; social worker presentation from our refugee and human rights clinic; social worker presentation from our center for transgender medicine and surgery.

If you have experienced resistance from your students to learning how to provide compassionate pastoral/spiritual care to transgendered patients, how have you met that resistance?
Yes, I have met resistance (mostly from students from Nigeria, Kenya, the Democratic Republic of Congo, the Philippines, students with more biblical-literalist approaches, Muslim students). I see their resistance as cultural, which they are currently separate from and trying desperately to hold on to while assaulted by both individual acts and systemic racism in the U.S. So, it is complex. They are experiencing tremendous loss themselves and are 'strangers in a strange land.' Religion is enculturated and so this often gets folded into the mix of their own adjustment to the U.S. So, I meet this complexity by empathizing with their loss, their experiences of racism, the ongoing trauma they experience and for a good many of them, the trauma they witnessed or were subjected to in their countries of origin. My hope is that by them experiencing empathy, they will be more likely to extend it even when it stretches their theology. In addition, I emphasize that I want them to be successful as a chaplain in *this* culture. Also, by incorporating this education within the context of understanding dominant power structures, many begin to see this is a systemic problem similar to racism or gender inequality which they themselves experience. The current political and right-wing religious rhetoric and behavior and policy changes are having an impact on their lives, too.

Do you, as part of the spiritual care team, teach your colleagues how to cultivate compassion for transgender patients? If yes, how?
This is something we all do together as a department. The hospital also provides training.

- **Please comment on my proposed method for cultivating compassion within a hospital setting for transgender patients (not necessarily in order of importance):**

- Take time to become familiar with one's own experiences in perpetrating religious discrimination.
- Read the U.S. Constitution and President Trump's executive orders and policy changes and recommendations regarding religious freedom to become aware of the political situation transgender people face.
- Become familiar with religious texts that support religious discrimination against transgender people.
- Support transgender people organizing themselves to have a collective voice and presence in society.
- Become advocates for compassion within and outside your healthcare institution.
- Identify other healthcare organizations throughout the country that will host you for conversations about the U.S. Constitution and religious discrimination against transgender people in healthcare settings. These conversations would involve at least two transgender spiritual leaders who will begin with a dialogue between themselves, then open the discussion to others, with instructions that people should be willing to take risks to be vulnerable in the spirit of liberating themselves from religiously based discrimination.
- Promote spiritual practices that help people become liberated from delusions of a separate self (mindful meditation, prayer, and service are options).
- Help health care workers understand what it means for health care workers to be engaged with people who are transitioning away from cisgender and how that engagement promotes their spiritual growth.
- Advocate for health care workers to take personal time for spiritual renewal with regular spiritual retreat practice and pilgrimages.
- Promote non-dualism and mutual interdependence.
- Demythologize entitlements around who receives and deserves healthcare.
- Demythologize religious supremacies.
- Advocate for healthcare systems for all in need regardless of income or religious beliefs.
- Shock and deconstruct the system by telling the truth when they see discrimination, refusing to participate in discrimination, supporting their colleagues who do not want to discriminate and engage in the work of integrating compassion and nondiscrimination throughout the healthcare organization.

  – Consider including U.S. Constitutional awareness as part of the
    CPE curriculum.

In response to my request for feedback on my proposed method, Rev. Dr.
Gould wrote, "There are many good ideas here. I hadn't considered
incorporating U.S Constitution awareness and current executive orders/
policy changes into our curriculum, and I'll need to think about it a little
more. BMC is a safety-net hospital that serves all patients regardless of
ability to pay, so that means many of our patients (including trans patients)
have fewer resources to manage the psychological/social stressors that
come from living on the margins of society."

Rev. Dr. Gould trains chaplain interns (who work for 11–22 weeks, as
opposed to residents who work full-time for one year) from many countries. Because interns train for shorter periods of time, Gould reports, "It's
really just about getting the [basic] principles of [spiritual care] down and
working within these principles to make decisions." When it comes to
helping interns cultivate compassion for transgender patients, she notes
that interns who come from countries outside the United States, Muslims,
and students with a "more biblical-literalist approach" demonstrate the
greatest initial resistance to caring for transgender patients. For those
interns, trans culture is not a part of their national culture. In the case of
scriptural literalists, some believe they are required to separate themselves
from US culture, which, according to Gould is "code for, 'Well, we don't
accept gay, lesbian, bisexual, transgender stuff anyway.' I think that's just
kind of a code way of saying that I think there are other kinds of hidden
codes that I may not even pick up on. 'Well, in my church we don't accept
the things in culture.' And, of course, quoting, just for gay and lesbian
stuff, the passages in Leviticus, household codes, all those things." Gould
cites one Nigerian Catholic student as an example. She says,

One of my CPE students, a Nigerian Catholic priest, showed me a video
that a friend of his had sent him from Nigeria of a public humiliation of a
man who somehow was known to be gay. This man was being dragged
through the streets with chants and jeering, cheering from the crowds, people throwing things at him, and people coming up and spitting on him.
Really public humiliation. I was curious about the pastoral response to this
public humiliation from the Catholic Church. This student shared that there
isn't a pastoral response from the church and priests are encouraged not to
get involved. My curiosity about the church's lack of response opened the

conversation about LGBT issues and how complex these issues are for students, especially those coming from other countries studying here.

Gould has worked at Boston Medical Center for 16 years. She has engaged in the educational programs on transgender care, including trainings by the Human Rights Campaign and Health Stream.[22] I asked her if she helps interns determine what is right or wrong or what brings about the good as it relates to spiritual care and transgender patients. She said, "My focus on ethics is in making what sometimes are called biomedical ethical decisions, not necessarily ethics from another perspective. We focus primarily on the principles of ethics, so patient autonomy, beneficence, malfeasance, those kinds of principles. And then surrogate decision making, health-care proxies, what to do when there's [no family] or friend and the patient has no health-care proxy. Those kinds of ethics within the realm of health care decision-making." Gould noted that many interns from countries outside the United States understand the collective decision-making function of the ethics committee over the privileging of autonomy that usually takes place between an individual patient and hospital staff.

Gould is the only Association for Clinical Pastoral Education CPE educator on staff at BMC. She calls on social workers to help educate spiritual care interns about trans patients. I asked why she needed the extra support.

Yetunde: Is it about the quantity of work, or is it about the quality of work, or just choices we have to make based on who we're working with?

Gould: I think it's about quantity in one way and the fact that I'm kind of a one-woman show here. I know that other supervisors have more administrative help, have other resources. I don't have a specific didactic on trans issues. I kind of leave that up to the clinic social worker to address.

Yetunde: And do you feel that the social worker addresses the spiritual issues as you would?

Gould: No, but then after she leaves, there's a chance to talk more about it. This can come up in group and it comes up with other presentations. When we visited a mosque, one of the students said, "What's the doctrine in Islam around lesbian, gay, bisexual, trans people?" It's kind of percolating and it gets expressed in different places as training progresses.

In addition to working with social workers, Gould teaches medical students about the role of religion and spirituality in health care in order to have a "downstream" effect on doctor-patient relationships. In her classes she talks about the LGBTQ community without segmenting the transgender community for special attention. One of her methods for helping students cultivate compassion for others is through a systems approach. What follows is a conversation I had with Dr. Gould regarding cultivating compassion among her students.

Yetunde: If we take the individual and the collective as concepts to consider, some would say there is no such thing as an individual self; we are all part of a bigger system or systems. Practices like mindfulness meditation, prayer, and service encourage recognition of this interdependency. Do you talk about such practices as ways of liberating interns from the delusion they are separate from others?

Gould: My goal, or one of my goals in Clinical Pastoral Education, is for students to discover that.

Yetunde: "That" being?

Gould: That we are more connected than we ever realized. But do I kind of forcefully put it out in the didactic? No. Do I make comments on verbatims[23] about it? Yes. When we discuss verbatims do I bring it up? Yes. Is my group-theory practice something that sustains this principle or this bullet point? Yes.

Yetunde: Can you explain that Jennie? What is that practice?

Gould: I'm not much [for] preaching that we are not separate beings. I think students come to that; at least I hope they do. In terms of group theory [that I use with CPE students, not medical students], I work from system-centered training theory, which was developed by Yvonne Agazarian, who, bless her heart, just died last year. Our practice in group is that when one person offers something, there's always someone else who will reflect back to them; sometimes that reflection is saying back immediately what that person has said in their own words and sometimes it's a kind of paraphrase. This helps interns begin to understand the power of accurately reflecting what a patient says as practice—reflective listening as a practice. The second part is to build on that reflection. So, somebody may talk about feeling overwhelmed. The way it would work in group is somebody else would respond, "Jane, you say you're feeling overwhelmed, you know, and I too have found myself feeling a lot more anxious these days, and it's because I am feeling more overwhelmed, too." The idea is for another person to reflect and also add something. The goal of this practice is to see that, although we may have kind of minute differences, there is a way we all collectively join. I think the group practice probably addresses the bullet point that you mentioned more than any kind of didactic that I would give or even any kind of experience. We have educational experiences, like visits to health care centers for the homeless, mosques, Buddhist temples. But it's really in group practice where we cultivate compassion. I see that also reflected in analysis and verbatims, so students will begin to say racially, ethnically, socio-culturally, economically, I am different from this patient, and, yet, I felt like she was speaking my life in some way. I think that awareness comes from the group practice.

In addition to cultivating compassion among her students, Rev. Dr. Gould guides her students toward being present with transgender patients by (1) empathizing with interns regarding their own cultural and scriptural-literalist struggles; (2) supplementing the lack of employee-only training with didactics from social workers and medical staff; (3) introducing interns to biomedical ethics; 4) attending to what is written in student verbatims; (4) refraining from being "preachy" about accepting transgender patients; (5) teaching religion and spirituality in health care to medical students; and (6) utilizing Yvonne Agazarian's systems work. Gould is a one-person CPE educator without administrative help. Her work, in a public hospital, is extremely demanding. She must create opportunities for collaboration across departments to ensure greater trans-competency among her interns.

Gould's colleague, Dr. Jennifer Siegel, medical director of BMC's Center for Transgender Medicine and Surgery (CTMS), also works with countless demands. I interviewed Dr. Siegel over the phone. While some of my recording of this conversation was indecipherable, I was able to record important information about the relationship between the CTMS and BMC's chaplaincy department.

Yetunde: How long has the Center for Transgender Medicine and Surgery been in existence?

Siegel: The Center for Transgender Medicine and Surgery dates to 2016. But I always say to people that the care and the art for providing for transgender patients dates back much, much longer at Boston Medical Center. We've long had numerous providers that were interested in competence in care. But what really came in the last two or three years is the organization of a really coherent culture. We call ourselves a virtual center that provides full-spectrum care across the lifespan for our transgender patients. As we organize ourselves medically, that has also been a good time for us to start to understand the broader hospital and health-system teams that we need to involve, including spiritual care.

Yetunde: I've been in clinical settings where there has been tension between the medical side and the spiritual side. I think I understand how some of those tensions manifest, so that's the backdrop for the question I'd like to pose about promoting spiritual care. Does the Center for Transgender Medicine and Surgery actually promote the spiritual care department, even though you don't know each other well yet?

Siegel: I would say right now, no. We do not do a good job of that whatsoever. However, while I don't think it comes from a place of tension with the spiritual care department, I think it totally comes from a place of overwhelm. I have a feeling now that we're all having this conversation. We probably will be promoting our spiritual care element once we clarify what we are doing with each other.

When I came to the realization that my presumption was incorrect, that the spiritual care department was not as fully integrated and supported at the CTMS as I had thought, I began asking different questions.

Yetunde: Is the Center for Transgender Medicine and Surgery using a spiritual care assessment tool?[24]

Siegel: Not a formal one, no. [There is no formal spiritual assessment tool specifically for transgender patients.]

Yetunde: Okay. Can you describe the informal one?

Siegel: I would say that we do, and this is super informal on the spiritual care end, take a fairly holistic intake when a patient contacts us. We take a biopsychosocial approach if we're going to use the older language about trying to understand the context of people's lives once we get to know them. So, are there questions that come up for people around religion and spirituality? Definitely. But are we doing that systematically? Absolutely not.[25]

Yetunde: What, if anything, do you think all hospital spiritual care departments, including chaplains, should know about working with transgender patients?

Siegel: Everybody in the hospital should know, regardless of whether they're a direct care provider, a therapist, a spiritual care provider, that they're in another dimension of the diversity that we're lucky enough to work with. It's important to recognize basics like checking in with people, making sure that we're asking what they want to be called, asking about their used name, using their used name, checking in with people about their used pronouns, things of that nature.

Yetunde: Would you say that many people who identify as transgender have financial obstacles?

Siegel: Yes, definitely. I'm not an expert on the financial side of things, but what I'm fairly familiar with is the reality that [there are] structural things, whether it's the uncompensated costs for transgender care, plus overall economic marginalization. I know these are generalizations, but ...[at] Boston Medical Center ... we try not to place economics as a barrier to taking care of people whatsoever. I'm thinking as a provider as much as the medical director right now: there is so much to think about when caring for transgender patients when you consider the medical issues at hand, when you think about family dynamics, oftentimes we know that there's a much higher rate of comorbid mental illness and all of the social pieces that we've already talked about.

Yetunde: Chaplains tend not to be educated in a deep way on psychology and mental illness and assessing mental illnesses. I think the curriculum should reflect more education in the area of mental illness. That will help make chaplains better collabora-

tive partners when working with doctors, but I'm just thinking out loud on that one.[26] Any thoughts about that?

Siegel: Definitely. We know from the U.S. Census and health surveys
that nearly 40 percent of transgender individuals experience
chronic, significant mental distress, which is way higher than
the general population. So much research is needed to clarify
this. It is important to know how spirituality interacts with
health more broadly, and to recognize that this is a tricky area
within the transgender [community where] people face so
much stigma and so much tension with their immediate fami-
lies and community structures. Having our spiritual care partners preparing themselves to engage in that and partner with
us around mental health for this population would be a huge
resource. We have a measure on the Massachusetts ballot for
November, specifically around transgender rights. Are you
aware of that?

Yetunde: Ballot measure three?

Siegel: Yes, which basically overturns public accommodations protections laws that we already have on the books. I can only
imagine the stress of having your benefits, or in the case of the
ballot initiative, your human rights to access of public spaces,
being debated. There must be incredible tensions. We see
that every day, the incredible tensions on affected populations—the stress related to that.

Dr. Siegel desires more collaboration with the Clinical Pastoral Education
(CPE) program, chaplaincy, and with Rev. Dr. Gould. Like Gould, however, Siegel and those who care for transgender patients at BMC's)CTMS
are overwhelmed with work. Gould, along with her interns, is a one-person CPE educator without administrative help, tasked with educating
interns across cultures and religions. Siegel, directing the CTMS, focuses
on medicine and a variety of other services, but spiritual care had not been
promoted and integrated. There is a gap. The Human Rights Campaign's
2018 Health Equity Index does not require the promotion or integration
of chaplaincy in order for a hospital to earn its highest score. Grossoehme
et. al.[27] found that spiritual struggle is high among the adolescent transgender population at Cincinnati Children's Hospital, where they did their
research. Siegel points out that the transgender population is understudied.

Religious-freedom-law literacy is not part of the CPE program, but Gould believes it should be, especially given her experiences witnessing fearful pregnant immigrant women coming to the hospital late for fear of deportation and miscarrying their babies as a result. Religious-freedom-law literacy and activism are low among the spiritual caregivers I have surveyed, and CPE educators, who are more aware of religious freedom laws are largely not educating their interns and residents about the laws that govern free religious exercise, free speech, and freedom from the governmental establishment of a "church." As the US Executive Office continues to make transgender people their sacrificial lambs in exchange for political support from some evangelical political organizations, precious resources are being taken from the hospitals. Spiritual caregivers need to redefine their roles and become public advocates when it comes to meeting the needs of transgender patients. We can be inspired by the life and work of black feminist Melissa Harris-Perry by cultivating hospitality in health care organizations, and, perhaps, keeping the doors of these organizations open to all in a radically cohabitating safe space way. One way to begin redefining what it means to be a spiritual caregiver is to experience one's own capacity for touching on a transgender capacity. Touching on one's own capacity for a transgender fluidity, what I call Relative Realm Gender Fluidity and Mystical Transcendental Transexuality, is the subject of Chap. 3.

NOTES

1. A. Walker, "Womanist," 19.
2. Yetunde, Pamela Ayo. "Black Lesbians to the Rescue! A Brief Correction with Implications for Womanist Christian Theology and Womanist Buddhology," *Religions*, 2017, 8(9), 175, 1 September 2017.
3. Others identified as Buddhist, Humanist, Jewish, Interfaith, and Latter-day Saint (Mormon).
4. I believe the majority of respondents were from Minnesota because I belong to a Minnesota chaplain list serve.
5. Other responses included: (1) Ability to build one's awareness of the power of the human nervous system and the effects of trauma on human resiliency and the ability to be in relationship. Developing tolerance for one's own inner activation; (2) The spiritual care needs of the patient/family; (3) Recognizing our humanness and the places in our own religious traditions that instruct us to love for those who are 'other'; (4) Increased self-awareness and understanding/respect for others.

6. Other ways to cultivate compassion for people outside one's religious group include: understanding the shared nature of the human experience; reading stories about people's journeys and challenges, travel/study; relationships; cultural humility education; study dialogue; inquiry; coping; experiencing the other in a mutually beneficial relationship; reading sacred texts from other traditions and seeking mentorship from people of other traditions; "Reflective Pause" is when students are asked to claim their own perspective and decision in using a reading/reflection.

7. https://www.thenation.com/article/progressive-bible-study/ (accessed March 3, 2018)

8. http://religiondispatches.org/melissa-harris-perry-lgbt-advocates-need-public-progressive-faith/ (accessed March 3, 2018)

9. https://juicyecumenism.com/2012/02/24/union-seminary-president-complains-on-msnbc-about-male-led-catholic-church/ (accessed March 3, 2018)

10. http://ajccenter.wfu.edu/wp-content/uploads/2012/12/syllabus-black-religion-political-thought-spring-2013-ajc.pdf (accessed March 3, 2018)

11. http://www.msnbc.com/melissa-harris-perry/rights-mississippi-now-subject-religion (accessed March 3, 2018)

12. Yetunde, "Black Lesbians to the Rescue!..."

13. Phillips, 19.

14. Chanequa Walker-Barnes, *Too Heavy A Yoke: Black Women and the Burden of Strength*, Cascade Books (Eugene, Oregon), 2014.

15. Ibid., 57.

16. http://religiondispatches.org/melissa-harris-perry-lgbt-advocates-need-public-progressive-faith/ (accessed March 5, 2018)

17. https://www.hrc.org/hei/search/massachusetts/boston-medical-center (Accessed September 6, 2018).

18. I define transcleansing as the combination of attempts on behalf of the US government to turn the nation against transpeople through discrimination, the withdrawal of services, impoverishment, the promotion of hate crimes against them, and the creation and enforcement of policies that do not recognize transpeople as a class of people worthy of equal protection under law.

19. https://www.bmc.org/center-transgender-medicine-and-surgery/clinical-services (Accessed August 28, 2018)

20. https://www.bmc.org/services/spiritual-care (Accessed August 28, 2018)

21. https://www.bmc.org/services/spiritual-care (Accessed August 28, 2018)

22. Health Stream is required of employees, but not CPE interns. In one of their blog post is states, in part:

While LGBTQ people experience the same diseases, injuries, and other health issues experienced by members of non-LGBTQ communities, we know that LGBTQ people experience these things differently. They have a higher risk of certain diseases and have historically faced discrimination within healthcare settings, which can create barriers to receiving appropriate care. In addition, clinical and non-clinical training frequently overlooks information on how to provide affirming care to the LGBTQ community. In another post, it is written, Get On the Same Page—Start with Definitions. The LGBTQ community is not homogeneous. The term LGBTQ represents a diverse group. It is important that both clinical and non-clinical staff understand the differences between the groups. The three very distinct aspects of sexual orientation–behavior, identity, and attraction are a good place to start. Bender states, "It's really crucial that we're able to differentiate these aspects of our patients' identity and not lump them together and make assumptions about one based on the other. We want to be careful to not assume that someone who is transgender for example, also identifies as lesbian or gay. Knowing someone's sexual orientation doesn't tell us their gender identity or vice versa." It is also important to understand that even the term LGBTQ is not inclusive of all members of this community, so we may hear patients using terms outside of these designations to describe themselves. Best Practices in Providing Affirming Care for LGBTQ Patients, https://www.healthstream.com/resources/blog/blog/2017/07/26/best-practices-in-providing-affirming-care-for-lgbtq-patients (Accessed January12, 2019).

23. Chaplains are trained to observe and listen very carefully. Their educators ask them to write about their pastoral/spiritual care visits word-for-word, as best as they can remember the encounter. This word-for-word "verbatim" is offered to the educator and/or peer group for consultation.

24. When I sent the interview transcripts to Gould and Siegel to ensure I understood their responses to my interviews, it was stated that a spiritual assessment tool is used for all patients, but there is not a spiritual assessment tool specifically for trans patients.

25. Given that Gould and Siegel do not use a formal spiritual assessment tool, after each interview, I sent them an email with the article "Screening for Spiritual Struggle in an Adolescent Transgender Clinic: Feasibility and Acceptability." In this article, the authors Grossoehme, Teeters, Jelinke, Dimitrious, and Conard found that there was a prevalence of spiritual struggle between 38 and 47 percent in the 115 adolescents and caregivers screened for spiritual struggles using the Rush Protocol and Negative R-COPE. *Journal of Heath Care Chaplaincy*, 22:54–66, 2016.

26. About the Trevor Project, https://www.thetrevorproject.org/about/#s m.00001mirt4urfgdposl9r0ro6y6yz (Accessed January 13, 2019).
27. Grossoehme, Teeters, Jelinke, Dimitrious, and Conard, "Screening for Spiritual Struggle in an Adolescent Transgender Clinic: Feasibility and Acceptability." *Journal of Heath Care Chaplaincy*, 22:54–66, 2016.

CHAPTER 3

Thich Nhat Hanh, the *Avatamsaka Sutra*, and Lady Mahamaya

Abstract Vietnamese Zen Buddhist monk Thich Nhat Hanh draws his cosmic, interdependent view of existence from *The Avatamsaka Sutra and The Lotus Sutra*. From *The Avatamsaka Sutra*, Nhat Hanh uses the writings on the Buddha's cosmic mother, Lady Mahamaya, throughout his teachings on one's ultimate responsibility toward one another—enlightenment. Nhat Hanh offers practices to imagine oneself (regardless of gender or reproductive functioning) giving birth to Buddhas and Bodhisattvas.

Keywords Thich Nhat Hanh • Avatamsaka Sutra • Womb • Mystical Transcendental Transsexuality • Relative Realm Gender Fluidity

> *Even my rabbi has internalized some of those negative things and has said some comments that wouldn't go over well if I didn't know that she meant well. Just about her experiences as well, because she actually she did part of her rabbinical training in a LGBTQ counseling office. And even then she had opinions of the people and I think some of those opinions have influenced how she looks at trans women. It's more of the same: people not understanding the difference between transvestism and transgenderism and mixing things up. I know that she's just trying to do what is right for me as opposed to actually meaning negative things and perpetuating bad thoughts.*
> *(Pichette, 34)*

© The Author(s) 2020
P. A. Yetunde, *Buddhist-Christian Dialogue, U.S. Law, and Womanist Theology for Transgender Spiritual Care*,
https://doi.org/10.1007/978-3-030-42560-9_3

61

In Chap. 1, I offered reflections on Buddhist-Christian dialogue, introduced Vietnamese Buddhist Zen Master Thich Nhat Hanh, and added Government, Law, and Psychology to Paul O. Ingram's Christian-Buddhist Interreligious Dialogue framework. In Chap. 2, I shared data from three surveys of spiritual care providers, including chaplains, pastoral counselors, and chaplain educators, and interviews with Rev. Dr. Gould and Dr. Seigel at Boston Medical Center (BMC), demonstrating a need for more religious freedom law literacy in the profession of spiritual care and what trans care competency looks like at BMC. In this chapter, I reintroduce Vietnamese Buddhist monk Thich Nhat Hanh and how I have come to read his mystical teachings on Lady Mahamaya, and how these teachings can contribute to deepening empathy with trans patients by touching on our own trans fluidity capacities. I begin by sharing my first encounter with Nhat Hanh's writings.

Franklin D. Roosevelt said that December 7, 1941, was "a date which will live in infamy," because on that day the United States was attacked by Japan.[1] I was born 20 years later. Two dates live in infamy for me: September 11, 2001, when the World Trade Center was destroyed by terrorists flying planes, and October 7, 2001, my 40th birthday and the day the United States retaliated against terrorism by dropping bombs in Afghanistan. October 7, 2001, is also the day I was introduced to Thich Nhat Hanh and his book *Touching Peace: Practicing the Art of Mindful Living*. I was not looking for Buddhism, but I was looking for peace of mind and body. Watching the bombings on a large-screen television at the Tucson airport as lines of uneasy people were lengthening, as nervous chatter was increasing, as unsettled crowds were forming around the television, made me feel an anxiety I had never felt before. Though I was determined not to live in fear and planned to board a plane bound for home, all flights were grounded that day. I took a bus instead.

I began to wonder what would happen next. My wonder turned to worry, then to fear as US President George W. Bush began to ready his nation for retaliation. We were at war, and I was turning 40. The pride and joy at turning 40 turned to existential angst, so I asked my friends to help me find "peace of mind." My friend Dianne Jacob, a Jewish woman who did not and does not practice Buddhism, gave me Nhat Hanh's book. I was more than ready to "touch peace," but I knew nothing about mindfulness. In the introduction, Nhat Hanh writes, "We don't need to wish our friends, 'Peace be with you.' Peace is already with them. We only need to help them cultivate the habit of touching peace in every moment."[2] I was attending an Episcopal church at the time I received this Buddhist book. In Episcopal churches we say, "Peace be with you," as if peace were dependent only upon external forces. Nhat Hanh's words struck me as true, or at least desirable. I wanted to feel peace no matter what the United States did in retaliation and no matter what others did to the United States in retaliation. I read on. Nhat Hanh offers a mindfulness exercise (in summary):

Breathing in and out, I know I am doing so. As I do so, I see myself as a fresh flower, as a solid mountain, as still water reflecting reality, and as free space.[3]

I tried it. For a few moments I felt free of anxiety. Since then, I have meditated almost every day. Following that first reading of *Touching Peace* in 2001, I read at least 20 other books by Nhat Hanh. In 2008, I donated my Nhat Hanh collection to a prison project. I purchased Nhat Hanh's recorded dharma talks, *The Ultimate Dimension: An Advanced Dharma Retreat on the Avatamsaka and Lotus Sutras*, in 2004. I thought I was "advanced" enough in my practice and study to be brought to a different level. In retrospect, I was not that advanced. I thought I knew what Nhat Hanh's writings were about until I listened to *The Ultimate Dimension* again at a personal four-day silent retreat in July 2018. This was the fourth time since 2004 that I had listened to the retreat recordings. What is the ultimate dimension of the *Avatamsaka Sutra*, the main subject of the recorded retreat?

If one enters a Zen Buddhist practice center or temple, a Shambhala Center, or a Tibetan Buddhist center or temple, one may hear practitioners chanting the *Heart Sutra*. Walking into a Soka Gakki center, one may hear practitioners chanting *Namo Renge Kyo*, a distillation of the *Lotus Sutra*. Many Buddhist practitioners have probably heard of the *Diamond Sutra*. Nhat Hanh says of the *Avatamsaka Sutra*, "The *Avatamsaka Sutra* is the greatest poem I have ever touched, experienced"[4] Yet, despite having authored more than 100 books, including a sizeable collection of nine sutra commentaries,[5] Nhat Hanh has not written a single book dedicated to commentary on the *Avatamsaka Sutra*. I argue that his body of work, taken together, is a multipart commentary on the *Avatamsaka Sutra*, written in bite-sized pieces for Western consumption. The purpose of this chapter is not to provide much written commentary on the sutra, but to offer how Nhat Hanh's teachings from his recorded retreat, along with other sources, may inspire pastoral and spiritual caregivers to widen the field of spiritual and pastoral care for transgender hospital patients and gently invite us to touch on our own trans identity capacities.

Before entering that discussion, it is important to understand why Nhat Hanh holds the *Avatamsaka Sutra* in the highest esteem. Nhat Hanh says,

> When I became a novice at the age of sixteen and a half, I was already introduced to the practice of the *Avatamsaka* but I didn't know.[6] The first book I was given to learn to study is called *The Verses for Daily Practice of Mindfulness*, many dozens of short poems that I had to memorize for the practice of mindfulness in my daily life. When I take the water and wash my hand, there is a poem for me to practice. Four lines for you to breathe in, breathe out, breathe in, breathe out while you wash your hands. Taking the water to wash my hands, I vow that everyone has pure hands capable of handling the Buddha's dharma. There are many poems like that for your practice. And most of those poems in that little book came from the *Avatamsaka*. I did not know until several years later. So, verses for mindful practice begin by the *Avatamsaka Sutra*.[7]

The poems, which Nhat Hanh calls gathas, include,

> 2. Taking the First Step of the Day
> ...Each mindful step
> Reveals the wondrous *Dharmakaya*[8]

> 3. Opening the Window
> ...Opening the window,
> I look out onto the *Dharmakaya*.[9]

Nhat Hanh, at the age of 16, begins to live his life in a monastery, repeating these gathas every morning, imagining himself and thinking of himself as an observer of the *Dharmakaya*. The *Dharmakaya* is a spiritual "body" of "truth" or "reality" of unnamed elements and energies that produce physical manifestations of Buddhas with human bodies. The *Dharmakaya* cannot be seen with the human eye, therefore faith and imagination are required.

> 4. Turning on the Light
> ...mindfulness is the light[10]

The Avatamsaka realm is full of light.

> 8. Using the Toilet
>   Defiled or immaculate…
>   The reality of interbeing is unsurpassed.[11]

The *Avatamsaka Sutra* that Nhat Hanh wants Westerners to understand, embrace, and practice is largely concerned with non-duality, interbeing, and interpenetration.

> 10. Bathing
>   Unborn and indestructible…
>   lie in the wonderful nature of the *Dharmadhatu*.[12]

The Avatamsaka world is described as limitless. The *Dharmadhatu* is the ultimate dimension. When practicing mindfulness deeply, it is said that one can experience one greater body, the *Dharmakaya*, as *Dharmadhatu* in a "place" beyond description and limitations while engaged in everyday activities.

> 11. Washing Your Body
>   The universe is perfumed with flowers[13]

Flowers are a central motif in the Avatamsaka world and in Nhat Hanh's teachings. Many of Nhat Hanh's publications include depictions of flowers, including lotuses, which appear frequently in the *Avatamsaka Sutra*.

> 15. Morning Meditation
>   The Dharmakaya is bringing morning light[14]

> 17. Lighting a Candle
>   offering the light to countless Buddhas[15]

There are countless Buddhas and bodhisattvas in the Avatamsaka world.

> 18. Offering Incense
>   May we and all beings be companions
>   Of Buddhas and bodhisattvas[16]

In the Avatamsaka world, those on the path to enlightenment are instructed to be disciples of buddhas and bodhisattvas.

Nhat Hanh's ministry, through his writings, monasteries, liturgies, and dharma talks, invites us to imagine ourselves as citizens of the cosmos. As citizens of the cosmos, we see that we come from nowhere in particular, even though we were once in our mothers' wombs, and we will not go anywhere in particular after our bodies die.

> 30. Serving Food
> ...I see clearly
> the presence of the entire universe[17]

The rich, multilayered, and overwhelming imagery of the *Avatamsaka Sutra* is an unrelenting treatise on how everything in existence is part of everything else in existence, whether manifested in a physical form that can be conceived of by the senses or not.

> 33. Beginning to Eat
> With the fourth mouthful, I practice equal love for
> all beings.[18]

In the Avatamsaka world, no one is discriminated against because the mind's tendency to discriminate has been eliminated through the varieties of spiritual practices and devotion to the buddhas and bodhisattvas.

> 46. Planting
> I entrust myself to Earth;
> Earth entrusts herself to me,
> I entrust myself to Buddha;
> Buddha entrusts *herself* to me [italics mine].[19]

In the Avatamsaka world, Buddhas and bodhisattvas are not limited to gender designations.

Nhat Hanh has given his students the *Avatamsaka Sutra* in these gathas and in many other ways without many of us, I venture most of us, ever knowing. He didn't know, at 16, that the gathas he received were from the *Avatamsaka Sutra*. I didn't know at 40 that the first meditation and visualization exercise I read in *Touching Peace* was inspired by the *Avatamsaka Sutra*. Perhaps Nhat Hanh thought it would be a distraction to mention to his intended audience that his inspiration arose from an extremely long Buddhist scripture.

The *Avatamsaka Sutra* is clearly a foundational scripture for Nhat Hanh. Thomas Cleary's *Avatamsaka Sutra* translation, *The Flower Ornament Scripture: A Translation of the Avatamsaka Sutra*,[20] contains 39 chapters and 1637 pages. Nhat Hanh includes commentary on this text near the end of his book, *Cultivating the Mind of Love*. In Nhat Hanh's recorded retreat, he explicitly mentions just two chapters from the *Avatamsaka Sutra*. In this retreat, Nhat Hanh talks about the Sumaya Heaven that is found in chapter 19.

> In chapter 19 of the *Avatamsaka Sutra*, there is a verse that I learned by heart at the age of sixteen. I didn't know it was from the *Avatamsaka Sutra*. It goes in my chanting book in the evening recitation that is the first four lines of a text that has the purpose of offering food, drink, sutras, loving-kindess to the hungry ghosts.[21] I learned to chant it as a novice, exactly fifty years ago. It means if people want really to know and to touch all buddhas of all times, they should contemplate the nature of the cosmos and realize that everything is mental construction. We build up our world by our collective mind. If our collective mind is deluded, we build hell. And if our collective mind is bright, is true, then we build up the Avatamsaka world.[22]

For Nhat Hanh, the *Avatamsaka Sutra* became the foundation of his worldview, marked by notions of interbeing and interpenetration, mysticism, transcendence, and "cosmicview." He continues to say about Sumaya Heaven,

> If people really want to know all buddhas of all times, they should contemplate the nature of the cosmos. All is mental construction. That is one of the basic teachings of the *Avatamsaka Sutra*. In the first gatha, in the first verse, the word elements here mean Buddha, fire, earth, water, and air. The elements have no distinctions; but with our deluded minds, with our delusions, we manufacture a lot of forms and then we are caught in it, like a painter who draws a ghost and who became afraid of the ghost he just drew. In the Palace of the Sumaya Heaven, we learn that nothing is born. There is no birth, there is no death, there is no coming, there is no going. There is nothing to attain, everything is there within, you don't have to run after anything at all.[23]

Chapter 19 of the *Avatamsaka Sutra* is a short description of what the Avatamsaka world is like:

The king of the Sumaya heaven, seeing from afar the Buddha coming, pro-
duced by magical powers a jewel lotus bank lion throne in his palace, with a
million tiers of decorations, wrapped in a million golden nets, covered with
a million drapes of flowers, ... drapes of garlands, ... drapes of perfumes, ...
drapes of jewels.[24]

Of the lion throne, Nhat Hanh says,

There are many lion seats, lion seats is a seat that is for buddhas and
bodhisattvas.
     Lion is an animal that has a very majestic way of walking and of sitting,
and lion seats are everywhere for you to enjoy sitting. In fact, in the
Avatamsaka realm every space, every spot you sit [in] becomes a lion seat
because buddhas and bodhisattvas have sat already there several times in the
past. So, when you sit down on that very spot, you get the energy of a
Buddha or a bodhisattva. And when you sit on a lion's seat, you get the
stability, you get the confidence, you no longer have low self-esteem. You
are stable, you enjoy sitting, and you continue to develop your joy, your
loving kindness, your happiness. Just sit anywhere.[25]

Visualization, a method frequently called upon by Nhat Hanh, is a way
for Buddhist practitioners to "purify their minds so they can look deeply
at the nature of reality."[26] One way to practice visualization is while walking. While walking, one might

see the presence of our mother in every cell of our body. Our body is a continuation of our mother's body. When you make a step you might say,
"Mother, walk with me," and suddenly you feel your mother walking with
you. Perhaps during her lifetime, she did not have a chance to walk in the
here and the now and to enjoy touching the earth like you have. So, suddenly compassion is born in you, because you can see your mother walking
with you. Not in your imagination, but as a reality. You can invite your
father and other people. You don't have to be with them physically in order
to touch their presence.[27]

Nhat Hanh says that practicing visualization in this way helps one transform the delusion of a separate self and affirms the reality that

what we touch, what we see, what we hear, is only a collective mental construction. We begin to understand that what we perceive is very much the
construct of our consciousness. To recognize *parakalpita* [collective mental

construction] as a mental construction is a step toward wisdom. And our practice will help us to see that the nature of the world as we see it is the nature of *parakalpita*, the nature of mental construction.[28]

Ultimately, visualization is not merely the work of imagination; visualization can be used to transform the delusion that there is a separation between one's self and the Buddha, one's self and other selves, and transform the delusion of independence. Nhat Hanh uses the word *paratantra* (leaning on each other)[29] as shorthand for saying that we are materially manifest because we are dependent on and interpenetrated with each other. The consequence of this dependency and interbeingness is a continuation of ourselves even when we are not materially manifest to the human eye. Another word Nhat Hanh uses is *parinispanna*, the nature of reality that is past the world of illusion. Nhat Hanh says not only can *parinispanna* be realized, but this entire practice of visualization can have psychological and behavioral benefits:

So, if you visualize like that, all negative complexes will vanish. All doubt that you can behave with the responsibility of a Buddha's mother will disappear and the Buddha in you will have a chance to manifest for yourself and for the world. And that is why visualization is a very important tool of meditation, of transformation. With a mind that is polluted by greed, by anger, you cannot do it well; that is why the purification of our thinking, of our mind, is very important.[30]

In Nhat Hanh's commentary on the *Avatamsaka Sutra*, he says he memorized the last lines of "Eulogies in the Palace of Sumaya Heaven." Nhat Hanh writes,

If people want to know
all Buddhas of all times,
they should contemplate the nature of the cosmos:
All is but mental construction,
It's like a painter
spreading various colors.
Delusion grasps different forms,
but the elements have no distinction,
In the elements, there is no form,
and no form in the elements.
And yet apart from the elements,

no form can be found.
In the mind is no painting.
In painting there is no mind.
Yet not apart from the mind
is any painting to be found.[31]

Nhat Hanh clearly finds the *Avatamsaka Sutra* beautiful. He explains that the Buddha referenced in the sutra is a person, even more than a person (*dharmakaya*),[32] and he offers an alternate name used for the Buddha, which is Vairochana, "the eternal Buddha of the ultimate dimension."[33] Hahn believes Vairochana and the Holy Spirit in Christianity are one:

> One day I asked a Catholic monk in Rome, "What is the Holy Spirit?" He said, "The Holy Spirit is the energy sent by God." I said, "That's wonderful" and asked, "Is that energy called Holy Spirit that animate person called Jesus Christ?" He said, "Yes." Without the energy Jesus could not be able to be there to acknowledge our presence, to touch us, to love us, to heal us. With the energy called the Holy Spirit you can perform miracles.[34]

In the Avatamsaka world, one can become a bodhisattva—a person who forsakes their own salvation in order to help others find liberation, no matter how many lifetimes it takes.[35] There are flowers representing inter-being, oceans of merit, happiness, vows, jewels of insight.[36] Indra's net of jewels represents "the infinite variety of interactions and intersections of all things."[37] There are clouds that rain (representing happiness),[38] lion seats (like royal thrones for those committed to mindful practice),[39] and para-sols that "represent the warmth and enjoyment of the mindfulness we are dwelling in."[40] Ultimately, Nhat Hanh conveys that

> The miracle is possible because of insight into the nature of interbeing. If you really touch one flower deeply, you touch the whole cosmos. The cosmos is neither one nor many. When you touch one, you touch many, and when you touch many, you touch one. Like Shakyamuni Buddha, you can be everywhere at the same time. Think of your child or your beloved touching you now. Look more deeply, and you will see yourself as multitudes penetrating everywhere, interbeing with everyone and everything.[41]

And if you take the whole of Nhat Hanh's teachings (if that's possible) and his recurring themes, you will know that Nhat Hanh's life's work has been concentrated upon transforming the mundane world as we think we know it "into the world of Avatamsaka."[42]

In the *Ultimate Dimension* retreat, Nhat Hanh also references the last chapter of the *Avatamsaka Sutra*, "Entry into the Realm of Reality." Listening to the retreat again in 2018, I heard something from this last chapter that didn't make an impression on me the first three times I heard it—Nhat Hanh's talks on Lady Mahamaya, the mystical mother of buddhas. Nhat Hanh says,

> In chapter 36 of the *Avatamsaka Sutra*, there is the story of a young man whose name is Sudhana. He has entered the realm of Avatamsaka by the practice of bowing down to the earth and emptying himself. Suddenly, he looks up and sees Lady Mahamaya sitting there and smiling. These are some of the things the lady told him: "Siddhartha was accompanied by so many buddhas and bodhisattvas and they were about to enter my body into my womb. I told myself how could that many buddhas and bodhisattvas enter into my tiny womb, but before I could do or say anything all of them entered into my body very easily and sometime later there are countless bodhisattvas come to me, they wanted to know whether Siddhartha [the historical Buddha's birth name] is comfortable in me, they wanted to enter my body as well. I did not have the time to say anything, all of them enter into me." One thing enters everything, and everything enters into one thing. That is the teaching of the *Avatamsaka*. In the cosmos, in the flower, the whole cosmos can be touched. That is what you see in the Avatamsaka realm, because you practice deep looking and you enter the nature of inter-being. This is because that is.[43]

Nhat Hanh is considered a Zen master; he is also masterful at making ancient, arcane, and opaque Mahayana scriptures (and Christian scriptures, too) accessible to everyday Western thinkers. Consider this passage about Lady Maya in Cleary's translation:

> Then Sudhana turning to go to Lady Maya, having attained knowledge from investigation of the sphere of Buddhahood, thought to himself, "How can I meet, associate with, and learn from spiritual benefactors whose senses are detached from all worlds, who do not abide anywhere, whose bodies are beyond all attachments, who have set out on the unimpeded path, who have purified the spiritual body, who skillfully project bodily forms by the illusion of physical action, who observe the world as being within the illusion of physical action, who observe the world as being within the illusion of knowledge, who are physical embodiments of vows, whose bodies are made of mind by the power of Buddha, whose bodies are not born and do not perish."[44]

And it goes on for another several lines before the reader encounters the end of the sentence. The juxtaposition of Nhat Hanh's transcript from an oral dharma talk and Cleary's written translation is not meant for compari son to determine who transmits the dharma better, but to illustrate what it takes to convey the Avatamsaka in English, orally, as an inspiration to Westerners. As to Lady Maya giving birth, Cleary writes,

> Then, as Lady Maya leaned against the holy fig tree, all the world rulers, the gods and goddesses of the realm of desire, the gods and goddesses of the realm of form, and all the other beings who had gathered there to make offerings to the enlightening being were bathed in the glorious radiance of Maya's body, and their arrays of offerings were also illumined thereby; and all the lights in the billion-world universe were eclipsed by Maya's light. ... Then everything in this universe was seen reflected in the abdomen of Lady Maya, and in all the worlds in the universe, at the foot of trees in groves in the capitals of the southern continents Lady Maya appeared just as she did in the Lumbini grove, surrounded by all the world leaders as she was about to give birth to the enlightening being ... And in each of those lifetimes, Lady Maya was the mother of the enlightening beings. And all the bodies of the enlightening being were seen as a magical reflection in the pores of Lady Maya. ... Then, when the time for the birth of the enlightening being had come, the diamond ground in front of Lady Maya split and a great jewel lotus called Calyx Arrayed with All Jewels emerged. ... Maya is the mother of the Buddha Vairocana.[45]

For many Westerners, I suspect, reading Cleary's translation will not be inspiring in the way Nhat Hanh wants the sutra to inspire. It is full of "unrealistic" imagery and images, it is fantasy and fantastical, it is irrational, and perhaps unrealizable for most practitioners. The Lady Maya image and archetype (mother giving birth to divine beings, like Mary giving birth to Jesus without having had sexual intercourse) might even be offensive to people of feminist and womanist leanings. (How can it be inspiring to have absolutely no agency in permitting or not permitting bodhisattvas entering one's womb?) On the other hand, from an academic perspective, there can be no real appreciation of the sutra without reading portions of it, and there is no full appreciation of Nhat Hanh's oral transmission without hearing it repeatedly. Nhat Hanh continues,

All worlds enter a pore, but at the same time, one point enters all worlds. In every world you will identify the presence of this pore, this hair hole. All beings' bodies enter the one body, one body enters all beings' bodies. If you touch your body, and you touch it deeply, you touch my body, you touch the body of everyone else. If you take good care of your body, you take care of all of us. If you kill yourself, you kill all of us. This is the teaching of the *Avatamsaka Sutra*. So, if you are mindful in eating and drinking and living your daily life, you take care of all of us because all bodies are in your body. I had said yesterday that if you are a woman, whether you are ten or twenty or forty, be sure that all of us are your children. If you don't behave, if you are unhappy, that's because of you. You have to take good care of yourself, you have to take good care of us, you are Lady Mahamaya, you are the mother of all buddhas.[46]

It is not possible to know from listening to the recordings why Nhat Hanh makes such a sexist appeal, especially when his writings do not support this view and especially when we consider that Sudhana sought out Maya for her advice and became her temporary disciple. Cleary writes,

She boldly considered and carried out all the undertakings of enlightening beings; she had completed all the elements of development of the will for enlightenment; she was engaged in protecting all beings; she undertook to be the mother of all enlightening beings and buddhas.
 Beginning with these, Sudhana saw Lady Maya in as many ways as atoms in the continent: seeing her, he magically made his body as extensive as Lady Maya, and with this omnipresent body bowed to the ubiquitous Maya. As he was bowing, an infinite variety of concentrations entered into him.[47]

Sudhana rose to Maya's occasion, grew to her size in order to approach her, still bowing, and when he bowed, he received concentrations, or meditative mind states.
 When I heard these talks for the fourth time, I wondered if Nhat Hanh was really speaking about himself, visualizing his own "womb" giving birth to buddhas and bodhisattvas. When he talks about girls and women having the responsibility of taking care of others, being inspired by Lady Mahamaya, I wondered about the disconnect. Why can he imagine himself having a womb that gives birth to buddhas and bodhisattvas, but only encourages the girls and women at the retreat to identify with Lady Mahamaya and take on the responsibility of caring? In a 1997 dharma talk, Nhat Hahn says,

Not only did he [Sudhana] see that Lady Mahamaya is the mother of all buddhas, but he looked into himself and he saw that he is the father of all buddhas of the past, of the future, and of the present moment. And in Avatamsaka, all of us are pregnant with a buddha inside. Whether you are a gentleman or a lady, you are pregnant with a buddha inside, and you are happy. You don't try to look for anything else because you know that buddha-nature is within you. You know that the Kingdom of God is within you.[48]

In an article based on dharma talks from 2004, Nhat Hanh asks,

Who is Mahamaya, the mother of the Buddha? Is that someone outside of you? Or is she you? Because all of us carry in our womb a Buddha. The Buddha Shakyamuni said, "You are a Buddha. There is a baby Buddha in each of you. Whether you are a lady or a gentleman, you carry within yourself a Buddha." Mahamaya is hope. Is she outside in objective reality or is she inside ourselves? So, if you visualize like that, all negative complexes will vanish. All doubt that you can behave with the responsibility of a Buddha's mother will disappear and the Buddha in you will have a chance to manifest for yourself and for the world. And that is why visualization is a very important tool of meditation, of transformation.[49]

In a 2012 *Avatamsaka* talk, Nhat Hanh says,

This story gives us a lot of insight, the feeling that you're large, you contain multitudes—a place for Buddha and millions and millions of bodhisattvas— means you have a lot of freedom. A person who is happy is a person who has a lot of space inside of him or her and around him and around her and that is the feeling of Mahamaya. But that freedom without space one person cannot be happy and what to do to help without a lot of space in your heart and around you. The kind of love that is taught by the Buddha has no frontier.[50]

Nhat Hanh uses pregnancy, giving birth, and rebirth, as motifs not just for Buddhist practitioners, but for Christians too. At his 1996 Christmas retreat at his monastery, Plum Village, in France, he said,

To me, it is possible for us to help the child within us to be reborn again and again, because the spirit of the child is the Holy Spirit, it is the spirit of the Buddha. There is no discrimination. A child is always able to live in the present moment. A child can also be free of worries and fear about the future. Therefore, it is very important for us to practice in such a way that the child in us can be reborn. Let the child be born to us.[51]

Nhat Hanh continued, "We celebrate Christmas. We celebrate the birth of a child. But we have to look into ourselves. There is a child in us to be born. Our practice is to allow the child to be born every moment of our daily life."[52] The concept, thoughts, visualizations of giving birth are central to Nhat Hanh's way of bringing his listeners, readers, and followers into a birth-giving sense of themselves.

Nhat Hanh's interpretation of the stories of Lady Mahamaya in the *Avatamsaka Sutra*, accompanied by his visualization instructions, are what I call Mystical Transcendental Transsexuality (MTT). When practiced effectively, MTT creates the conditions that allow for the experience of Relative Realm Gender Fluidity (RRGF), or the potential for cisgender chaplains to grow in empathy with and compassion for transgender hospital patients.

Mystical Transcendental Transexuality is what happens when Sudhana, a boy, visualizes Lady Mahamaya. Nhat Hanh says,

> Who is Mahamaya, the mother of the Buddha? Is that someone outside of you? Or is she you? Because all of us carry in our womb a Buddha. Mahamaya is very careful because she knows that she carries a Buddha within. Everything she eats, everything she drinks, everything she does, every film she watches— she knows that it will have an effect on her child. The Buddha Shakyamuni said, "You are a Buddha. There is a baby Buddha in each of you. Whether you are a lady or a gentleman, you carry within yourself a Buddha." We also carry a Buddha, but we are not as careful as Mahamaya in our way of eating, drinking, smoking, worry, projecting, and so on. We are not responsible mothers of the Buddha.[53]

The practice of visualization serves as a mode of contacting other worlds, the worlds of the *Avamtasaka*, where a multitude of buddhas, bodhisattvas, Lady Mahamaya, and Sudhana reside. Lady Mahamaya and her baby buddha have no births and no deaths. Lady Mahamaya's body, the baby buddha's body, and the bodhisattvas are all without boundaries—they interpenetrate one another. The bodhisattvas do not wait until Lady Mahamaya decides whether they can enter her womb. Her womb is not really inside her body, and therefore it can be in any body. We are seeds of awakening and we plant and fertilize seeds of awakening in others as Lady Mahamaya did to Sudhana by blessing him with the transmission of concentrations or deep meditative mind states. If we can visualize ourselves having "wombs," for the incubation of awakening, and visualize ourselves as seeds or "sperm" or fertilizer to contribute to the growth of awakening beings, we can begin transforming our relationships with others to become true spiritual friends.

Nhat Hanh utilizes themes of mothering, the womb, and mindfulness as ways to inspire people to act like Lady Mahamaya:

> The Buddha described the seed of mindfulness that is in each of us as the "womb of the Buddha" (*tathagatagarbha*). We are all mothers of the Buddha because we are all pregnant with the potential for awakening. If we know how to take care of our baby Buddha by practicing mindfulness in our daily lives, one day the Enlightened One will reveal himself or herself to us.[54]

The "parent" need not be "female" to visualize being pregnant, and the baby buddha need not be conceived of as "male."

Nhat Hanh's teachings on Lady Mahamaya that reference gender fluidity are echoed in references he makes to the gender of the bodhisattva Avalokiteshvara, an important archetypal deity in Mahayana Buddhism:

> There is a bodhisattva called Avalokiteshvara. *She* is very talented, skillful in listening. Quan The Am is her name in Vietnamese, Quanyin in Chinese—it means listening deeply to the sound of the world. And, of course, the energy that helps *him* to listen deeply is the energy of mindfulness. If *she he* [sounds like Nhat Hanh is correcting himself] is not there, how could he listen. Avalokiteshvara is using *his* energy of mindfulness in order to listen [italics mine].[55]

It makes sense that Nhat Hanh would refer to this bodhisattva alternately as both she and he, given that he is aware of many Mahayana Buddhist traditions in many countries and teaches throughout the world. Avalokiteshvara is known by different names in different countries[56] and is understood to be the bodhisattva that can change forms, including gender forms. A bodhisattva that can change forms is of great symbolic and creative significance to Nhat Hanh and his monastic and lay orders. Those ordained into the monastic order engage in a ritual called Recitation of Bodhisattva Avalokiteshvara's Name. During the recitation of the bodhisattva's name, purified water is sprinkled with a willow branch or flower over the head of the ordinee, or around the perimeter of the hall or building to be blessed. The recitation includes repeating Avalokiteshvara's name 21 times.

In addition to Nhat Hanh's reverence for Lady Mahamaya and bodhisattva Avalokiteshvara, he refers to the Buddha as *she* in his Planting Gatha:

46. Planting
    I entrust myself to Earth;
    Earth entrusts herself to me,
    I entrust myself to Buddha;
    Buddha entrusts *herself* to me [italics mine].[57]

Nhat Hanh has made it a subtle project to encourage his students to
look deeply within and beyond gender concepts of Buddha. He writes
regarding his own embrace of Buddhism and Christianity, "They [Jesus
and Buddha] are real brothers, they are real sisters within me."[58]

Lady Mahamaya, Avalokiteshvara, and Buddha as herself, as a sister, is a
spirituality that contributes to Mystical Transcendental Transsexuality
(MTT), holding the potential for chaplains who cling tightly to their perceived gender constructions to relax their grasps on such perceptions, just
long enough to experience Relative Realm Gender Fluidity (RRGF). They
do this by imagining the self as possessing the suchness of another gender
or genders in order to step into the shoes, at least momentarily, of transgender patients. In conversations with Christians who practice Buddhism,
or former Christians who identify as Buddhists, they have talked about
how Buddhism helps them become more loving and compassionate.
Buddhist-inspired MTT and RRGF are spiritual visualization practices
that help practitioners "to not be of this world," to transcend the world of
discriminatory laws, policies, and practices against trans people that support hatred and indifference and result in the impoverishment of health
care systems. In Chap. 5, I explore how Buddhist and Christian dialogue
within chaplaincy may contribute to the creation of hate-free zones within
health care settings. Having discussed Buddhist-Christian dialogue, the
need for spiritual caregivers to become politically involved for the welfare
of trans people, and Nhat Hanh's Buddhology as it relates to the
Avatamsaka Sutra and Lady Mahamaya, I turn to the subject of US religious freedom law because interreligious dialogue (without knowledge of
religious freedom law principles), data analysis, and spiritual practices,
even when combined, are not enough to prepare us to be effective public
advocates when the legal system, and trans citizens, are under attack.

NOTES

1. "A Date Which Will Live in Infamy": FDR Asks for a Declaration of War, http://historymatters.gmu.edu/d/5166/ (Accessed August 28, 2018).
2. Thich Nhat Hanh, *Touching Peace: Practicing the Art of Mindful Living* (Berkeley: Parallax Press, 1992), 9.
3. Ibid., 11–12.
4. Thich Nhat Hanh, *The Ultimate Dimension: An Advanced Dharma Retreat on the Avatamsaka and Lotus Sutras* (Boulder: Sounds True), Disc 6.
5. Thich Nhat Hahn, *Awakening of the Heart: Essential Buddhist Sutras and Commentaries* (Berkeley: Parallax Press) 2012.
6. Thich Nhat Hanh's monastery was Zen and Pure Land. Thich Nhat Hanh, *Living Buddha, Living Christ* (New York: Riverhead Books, 1995, 2007), 127.
7. Nhat Hanh, *The Ultimate Dimension*, Disc 2.
8. Thich Nhat Hahn, *Present Moment, Wonderful Moment: Mindfulness Verses for Daily Living* (Berkeley: Parallax Press, 2006), np.
9. Ibid., np.
10. Ibid., np.
11. Ibid., np.
12. Ibid., np.
13. Ibid., np.
14. Ibid., np.
15. Ibid., np.
16. Ibid., np.
17. Ibid., np.
18. Ibid., np.
19. Ibid., np.
20. Thomas Cleary, *The Flower Ornament Scripture: A Translation of The Avatamsaka Sutra* (Boulder: Shambhala Publications, Inc., 1993).
21. In the Offering to the Hungry Ghosts Ceremony, part 2. Recollection, it says, "Homage to the Buddhas and Bodhisattvas in the Avatamsaka Assembly." and it is repeated three times. In part 4. Recollection it says, "Homage to the Avatamsaka Sutra proclaimed by the Buddhas in all quarters…". In part 6. Verses of Offering there is a recitation to some of the tathagatas (suchness) in the Avatamsaka Sutra including Multiple Jewel, Jewel Victory, Wonderful Form Body, Extensive Body, Far from Fear, nectar of compassion, and Infinite Light, and in part 9. Sharing the Merit it states, "…May we be born now in the Pure Land within the heart of a lotus flower. In the moment when the lotus booms, we touch the reality of no-birth and no-death…" Thich Nhat Hanh, *Chanting from the Heart: Buddhist Ceremonies and Daily Practices* (Berkeley: Parallax Press, 2007), 196–201.

22. Nhat Hanh, *The Ultimate Dimension*, Disc 3.
23. Ibid., Disc 4.
24. Cleary, 438.
25. In Cleary's translation, the Buddhas in chapter 19 are: "The Buddha Renown, famed throughout the ten directions, The Buddha Jewel King, lamp of the world, The Buddha Joyful Eye, with unhindered vision, The Buddha Burning Lamp, lighting the world, the Buddha Benefactor, aid of the world, The Buddha Well Aware, who had no teacher, The Buddha Surpassing the Gods, a lamp in the world, The Buddha No Departure, hero of philosophy, The Buddha Unsurpassed, replete with all virtues, The Buddha Ascetic, benefitting the world.", 440.
26. Thich Nhat Hanh, "Dharma Talk: The Power of Visualization," *The Mindfulness Bell* #38 Winter/Spring 2005, https://www.mindfulnessbell. org/archive/2015/06/dharma-talk-the-power-of-visualization-2 (Accessed September 6, 2018).
27. Ibid.
28. Ibid.
29. Ibid.
30. Ibid.
31. Thich Nhat Hanh, *Cultivating the Mind of Love* (Berkeley: Parallax Press, 1996), 95.
32. Ibid.
33. Ibid., 85.
34. Nhat Hanh, *The Ultimate Dimension*, Disc 5.
35. Ibid.
36. Ibid., 86.
37. Ibid., 87.
38. Ibid.
39. Ibid., 87–88.
40. Ibid., 88.
41. Ibid., 89.
42. Ibid., 90.
43. Ibid., Disc Two.
44. Cleary, 1430.
45. Ibid., 1390–1393.
46. Nhat Hanh, *Ultimate Dimension*, Disc Four.
47. Cleary, 1435.
48. Thich Nhat Hanh, "All in One, One in All," https://sites.google.com/ site/tnhdhamma/Home/test-list/all-in-one-one-in-all (accessed August 28, 2018).
49. Thich Nhat Hanh, "Dharma Talk. The Power of Visualization," The Mindfulness Bell, #38 Winter/Spring 2005. https://www.mindfulnessbell.

org/archive/2015/06/dharma-talk-the-power-of-visualization-2 (accessed August 28, 2018).

50. Thich Nhat Hanh, "Avatamsaka Talk," https://tnhaudio.org/tag/avatamsaka-sutra/ (accessed August 21, 2018).

51. Thich Nhat Hanh, *Going Home: Jesus and Buddha as Brothers*, 67.

52. Ibid., 108.

53. Nhat Hanh, "Dharma Talk. The Power of Visualization," *The Mindfulness Bell*, #38 Winter/Spring 2005. https://www.mindfulnessbell.org/archive/2015/06/dharma-talk-the-power-of-visualization-2 (accessed August 28, 2018).

54. Nhat Hanh, *Living Buddha, Living Christ*, 40.

55. Nhat Hanh, *The Ultimate Dimension*, Disc Three.

56. "In *Macau, Hong Kong,* and *southern China* she is called Kwun Yum or Kun Yum. In *Japanese* she is called Kannon, Kan'on, or Kanzeon. In *Korea* she is called Gwan-eum or Gwanse-eum. In *Thailand* she is called Kuan Im, Phra Mae Kuan Im, or Chao Mae Kuan Im. In *Indonesian* she is called Kwan Im or Dewi Kwan Im. In *Vietnamese* she is called Quan Âm, Quán Thế Âm or Quán Thế Âm Bồ Tát. In *Khmer*, She is called "Preah Mae Kun Ci Iem." Guan Yin, https://simple.wikipedia.org/wiki/Guan_Yin) (Accessed September 9, 2018).

57. Ibid., np.

58. Nhat Hanh, *Going Home: Jesus and Buddha As Brothers*, Riverhead Books, 1999, 196.

CHAPTER 4

Think Like a Lawyer, Act Like a Chaplain

Abstract The US government, including the US Supreme Court, has considered the US Constitution, federal statutes, state statutes, and numerous cases related to religious freedom and chaplaincy. Many states have adopted their own religious freedom statutes in response to the court's limits on the Religious Freedom Restoration Act (RFRA) of 1993. Many states adopting their own RFRA-like statutes have attempted to legalize discrimination, in the name of religion, in many sectors of their state. There has also been resistance to state RFRAs from Corporate America. The Trump-Pence Administration changed policies within the Department of Health and Human Services (HHS) to reflect the spirit of anti-trans state RFRAs in health care settings.

Keywords First Amendment • US Constitution • US Supreme Court • Religious Freedom Restoration Act • *Masterpiece Cakeshop v. Colorado Civil Rights Commission* • Department of Health and Human Services (HHS) Office for Civil Rights Conscience and Religious Freedom Division (CRFD)

More than a third of 37 percent can't name any of the rights guaranteed under the First Amendment; only a quarter of Americans (26 percent) can name all three branches of government.

© The Author(s) 2020   81
P. A. Yetunde, *Buddhist-Christian Dialogue, U.S. Law, and Womanist Theology for Transgender Spiritual Care*,
https://Doi.org/10.1007/978-3-030-42560-9_4

(Americans Are Poorly Informed About Basic Constitutional Provisions. https://www.annenbergpublicpolicycenter.org/americans-are-poorly-informed-about-basic-constitutional-provisions/ (Accessed January 10, 2019))

As it relates to the First Amendment, all chaplain educators said they are aware of the rights in the First Amendment, but 69 percent said they do not educate their residents and interns about it. Seventy-five percent of chaplain educators surveyed do not educate their students about the Fourteenth Amendment's equal protection clause.

(Chaplain Educators and Religious Freedom Curriculum Survey, Fall 2018, Pamela Ayo Yetunde, Harvard Divinity School Post-Doctoral Fellowship project)

Are chaplains, pastoral counselors, and other spiritual caregivers who aspire to higher spiritual and religious laws interested in the rights and protections offered in the US Constitution and the judicial branches that were created to uphold and protect the rule of secular law? What do spiritual leaders bring to bear when conflicts arise between religious or spiritual law and secular law? As one who is law educated and practices and teaches in the field of pastoral care and counseling, I believe our experiences, studies, practices, and wisdom combine to inform our responses when accompanying those who suffer; together, they inform our responses in both our private lives and in our professional roles.

In the United States, a relatively violent country with an astoundingly high incarceration rate, we are still struggling to find and maintain democracy, civility, and freedom. But this cannot be accomplished through legislation alone. Taking civilization to the next level will require wise people and mystics to become versed in and protective of the laws that will lead us there. Without the wisdom of our imperfect founding fathers, we might be living in a theocracy, where privilege would be dependent upon one's allegiance to a particular belief system. That would not be America, land of the free. Wisdom tells us that human flourishing is best met when minority populations, those most vulnerable to the aggression of the majority, are seen, heard, and protected. Are we listening?

Aurora Jade Pichette is indeed listening to the stories of those who may not otherwise have found a forum. Pichette, a trans woman, social worker, and religious leader in Heathenry, composed a thesis[1] on the religious lives of six trans women: Oshunlade, a Lukumi practitioner; Tee, an Anglican; Kay who is Jewish; Andrea who is Christian; Kae who is Quaker; and Aurora Jade herself, a priestess and herald for the Procession of Nerthus at the Midgard Festival in the Heathen community. Throughout this text, the voices of these religious trans women will be included as a way of understanding their experiences of discrimination in their religious communities.

Kae describes discrimination against trans people in this way:

> I guess that was like for me a point where no matter how accepting people have been on face value, "we support you in this," I had at that point even forgiven people being confused about pronouns and not knowing what to do, and it being so hard for them and, being like, "Okay I can, I think this is [expletive omitted], but fine, you tell me that it is hard, but at least there is some acknowledgement here" ... despite all of that, this happened to one youth in particular: a boy ... came dressed up like a really, really dolled-up woman ... and then it became this whole thing that not only the campers were laughing at and making comments about really loudly and really openly, but then the staff started to do it, and this is staff I've been working with since I was thirteen. Some of these people I've grown up with and ... I'm still not being taken seriously in any way, despite having come out, despite what I have been wearing, my name change, all of this stuff.[2]

On religion, Kae says,

> [There are] so many reasons to be iffy about religion, because people do awful things in the name of religion or God. The institution of a church is used for social control and warps the teachings of any of the prophets or people who are seen to be prophets. It just takes the truth out of it and creates this, this power structure that has been responsible for mission work all over the world, the spread of deadly epidemics, teaching shame to indigenous people all over the world. And I think about how different religions flat-out hate gays and flat-out hate trans people. There are so many reasons, so many reasons for people to hate religion and to feel skeptical about it. I guess what feels unfortunate to me is this: that also means this cutting out spirituality, which is, I think, a failing.[3]

Others like Kae have much to say about how religion and spirituality operate in the lives of cisgender people, how they are used against trans people, and how they may help oppressed people cultivate resiliency.

Wisdom in law making may serve as a remedy to critiques like Kae's and may help this country live up to its democratic ideals. One way religions contribute to wisdom is through the work of chaplains. According to Winnifred Fallers Sullivan,

> By defining what they do as "spiritual" care, rather than as religion, chaplains also finesse the separation [of church and state] versus establishment [the government making a religion for its citizens to believe in and follow] problem. If spirituality is universal, then it is not divisive the way religious affiliation and association is and so its sponsorship and regulation arguably do not raise the same problems for public order as does the favoring of a particular religious community by the state.[4]

Chaplains do more than pray for the sick; they help moderate public order by attending more to the spiritual realm than to divisive religious beliefs, practices, and rituals. Chaplains dwell in liminal spaces, responsibly holding their own religious traditions, beliefs, and practices in ways that do not run afoul of the US Constitution's equal protection clause. They do this while simultaneously respecting the individuals they care for and honoring the ethics of their religious traditions. Importantly, chaplains are tasked with remaining aware of the codes of ethics for their professional affiliations while working within the ethical norms of their workplaces. There is much to hold in tension when working as a professional hospital chaplain in the United States.

The United States promotes responsible religious freedom, which, at its best, results in moral and ethical behaviors and increased overall satisfaction in life. Systems of government that deny choice of religion result in a loss of liberty. The United States is not a country of religious dictators, but a nation whose federal government is composed of three branches—legislative, executive, and judicial—and whose states are composed of their own branches of government (a governor, a legislature, and courts). Through these checks and balances, ideally, the fundamental human rights of all persons are protected. Under the Trump-Pence administration, the Executive Office has repeatedly accused the US Supreme Court and federal judges of political bias, the free press as dispensers of "fake news," and Congress has not kept the president, who declared a national emergency to divert billions of dollars from military spending to build a wall between the United States and Mexico, in check. The very system of checks and balances is mocked by the White House, and the small population of transgender people is scapegoated.

Approximately 1.4 million, or 0.6 percent, of Americans identify as transgender,[5] a very small minority. What is our obligation to this small minority of American citizens? Minority equal protection is about governing in civil, humane, and legitimately democratic ways. Jesus-based Christianity defies ways in which governmental powers dehumanize others and take up the responsibility of care, compassion, and justice. Listening to minorities is a way to learn how those in the majority really are governing and allows minority populations to engage in the transformation of democracy. I argue that pastoral and spiritual caregivers need to be involved in democratic institutions beyond voting; as educated, critically thinking spiritual leaders they hold the potential to wisely engage in the democratic process in ways that can contribute wisdom and compassion in the protection of minority rights while respecting religious freedom.

Unfortunately, many spiritual care professionals are not prepared for such critical involvement because seminary education and Clinical Pastoral Education (CPE) are typically not infused with legal education. Sullivan says,

> The U.S. chaplain, in particular, has come to instantiate the peculiar and shifting religious terrain framed by the religion clauses of the First Amendment to the U.S. Constitution; she operates at the intersection of the sacred and the secular, a broker responsible for ministering to the wandering souls of a globalized economy and a public harrowed by a politics of fear— while also effectively sacralizing the institutions of the contemporary world.[6]

Students don't tend to attend seminaries and divinity schools to receive a legal education. Law schools are for lawyers and seminaries are for religious leaders. Though some law schools and divinity schools offer joint programs in law and religion, most seminary students do not receive a legal education. Sullivan says,

> Very consistently across Christian seminaries, the degree requirements today include courses in basic Koine (New Testament) Greek and biblical Hebrew, biblical exegesis, church history, doctrinal theology, ethics, and practical theology, as well as courses in either cross-cultural contextualization or evangelism, depending on the orientation of the school.[7]

Given the consolidation of a coercive and threatening brand of power behind the current US president and his party, chaplains, the unseen, unheard, and unsung spiritual leaders of our time, need to be better educated in religious freedom law, as state religious freedom legislation continues to sweep the United States. For example, despite the fact that since 1791, the First Amendment of the US Constitution has protected religious freedoms, 224 years later, in 2015, 21 states passed their own religious freedom laws (inspired by the federal Religious Freedom Restoration Act of 1993 and Supreme Court cases *Employment Division v. Smith* and *Boerne v. Flores*).

Though there are many religious freedom cases, I will begin this discussion with *Katcoff v. Marsh*, a 1984 case that demonstrates a lack of strict separation between church and state, in particular between military chaplains and the federal government. The First Amendment states:

> Congress shall make no law respecting an establishment of religion, or prohibiting the free exercise thereof; or abridging the freedom of speech, or of the press; or the right of the people peaceably to assemble, and to petition the government for a redress of grievances.

In *Katcoff*, law students who were not in the US Army and were not chaplains sued the federal government, alleging a violation of the First Amendment's establishment clause by hiring military chaplains. They argued that the federal government was establishing a religion by hiring military chaplains. The Court found against the students, but before arriving at their conclusion, the court had to determine whether the students had standing, or the right to sue. The court found that the students, as tax payers, had the right to sue. The facts of the case were not in dispute. Congress, through federal statute 10 U.S.C. Section 3073 (1976), established army chaplaincy, paying salaries as well as paying for chaplain publications, retreats, and sacred objects. Chaplains' duties included holding religious services and offering religious education. Is this the establishment of a religion or an excessive entanglement between church and state?

Before entering the Court's decision, it is important for chaplains to reflect on what government "establishment" would entail and what a "religion" is. In establishing a military chaplaincy, did the federal government create a religion? Did it or does it promote Christianity? The Court said:

> A cleric who would become a Chaplain must first be approved by an ecclesiastical endorsing agency recognized by the Army. The endorsing agencies are not limited to the largest religious groups in the United States; in fact, according to defendants, there are 47 such agencies, representing 120 denominations.[8]

Given this evidence, the plaintiffs could not demonstrate that Congress and the US Army were establishing any particular religion. The Court noted that while the plaintiffs were concerned about the government establishing a religion, the defendant (the secretary of the army) was concerned about soldiers' free exercise of religion, especially while in combat.[9] The Court defined the issue as "Whether Congress, acting under its explicit constitutional authority to raise and support armies, has in carrying out that authority transgressed the equally explicit guarantee of individual rights contained in the Establishment Clause."[10] No matter how the plaintiff defines the issue, the Court can redefine it, in this case, by stating that the power of Congress is to raise and support an army *first* and in conjunction with individual rights to be free from the government establishing a religion. Both must be taken into consideration.

In order to address the issue, the Court applied the three-part test from the Supreme Court case *Lemon v. Kurtzman*:

1. The statute must have a secular legislative purpose;
2. its principal or primary effect must be one that neither advances nor inhibits religion;
3. the statute must not foster 'an excessive government entanglement with religion.'

The Court agreed with the defendants, who argued:

1. chaplaincy is necessary for good morale;
2. the First Amendment Free Exercise Clause requires the government to provide means of worship for Army personnel; and
3. voluntary chaplains cannot meet the needs of the U.S. Army, therefore the Army can support religious institutions [to arrive at their goals of supporting morale and free exercise of religion].[11]

It is important to note that the Army was not arguing for the right to compel soldiers and other personnel to change their religious beliefs, adopt beliefs, or exercise their beliefs or non-beliefs in particular ways. To do so would have been an infringement of the establishment clause. Also, had the Army only allowed Christians to be chaplains, that would have infringed on the free exercise clause. The court noted,

Affording an opportunity for worship without coercion preserves the religious neutrality of the Government. As the Court recognized in *Everson v. Board of Education* ... the First Amendment "requires the state to be a neutral in its relations with groups of religious believers and non-believers; it does not require the state to be their adversary. State power is no more to be used so as to handicap religions, than it is to favor them."[12]

Hospital chaplains, especially public-hospital chaplains, can take instruction from *Katcoff*, that chaplains, as government employees, should be religiously neutral, not using their pastoral or spiritual authority to be a religious adversary of the patient, regardless of the chaplain's religious beliefs. When working in a public hospital, a chaplain's obligation to patients and staff is not the same as it is in their particular places of worship. The chaplain working in a hospital funded by the government and hired by the hospital, is a government employee and should provide spiritual care so as not to implicate their employer, the government, as a religious adversary. The chaplain's role is to be one who makes it possible for the *responsible* exercise of religious freedom.

While not centering on chaplaincy or spiritual care, another opportunity for examining the complex nature of religious freedom litigation exists in the 1990 Supreme Court case *Employment Division, Department of Human Resources of Oregon v. Alfred L. Smith*. In this case, the Court found that the claimants, Native Americans who had used peyote as a religious practice while at their Native American Church, did not have the right to do so because the state of Oregon had made peyote use a crime. The claimants, exercising their supposed religious freedom, lost their jobs (they worked for a private drug rehabilitation organization) and were disqualified from receiving unemployment benefits. The Court defined the issue as such:

> This case requires us to decide whether the Free Exercise Clause of the First Amendment permits the State of Oregon to include religiously inspired peyote use within the reach of its general criminal prohibition on use of that drug, and thus permits the State to deny unemployment benefits to persons dismissed from their jobs because of such religiously inspired use.[13]

The Court decided that the state of Oregon had the power to criminalize peyote use. To arrive at that conclusion, the Court said, in part,

> Conscientious scruples have not, in the course of the long struggle for religious toleration, relieved the individual from obedience to a general law not aimed at the promotion or restriction of religious beliefs. The mere posses-

sion of religious convictions which contradict the relevant concerns of a political society does not relieve the citizen from the discharge of political responsibilities.[14]

That was 1940. A quotation that is particularly relevant for an anti-trans citizen Executive Office that attempts to use religion to thwart equal protection rights, is found in *Reynolds v. United States*:

> We rejected the claim that the criminal laws against polygamy could not be constitutionally applied to those whose religion commanded the practice. "Laws," we said, "are made for the government of actions, and while they cannot interfere with mere religious belief and options, *they may with practices...* Can a man excuse his practices to the contrary because of his religious belief? To permit this would be to make the professed doctrines of religious belief superior to the law of the land, and in effect to permit every citizen to become a law unto himself."[15]

In short, the government may interfere with religious practice. *Reynolds* was decided in 1879. Despite the fact that the claimants in the 1990 Oregon case used peyote in a sacramental way, in their church, not during work hours, and with no evidence cited that their peyote use negatively impacted their job performances or negatively undermined the confidence of those in treatment, the Supreme Court sided with the state of Oregon, or the rule of state law. Three years later, Congress passed the Restoration of Religious Freedom Act (RFRA). It is important to note the politically rhetorical phrasing of *restoring religious freedom*, which suggests that religious freedom had been lost or stolen and could be restored only through federal legislation.

To practice thinking like lawyers, chaplains would benefit by familiarizing themselves with legislation pertaining to religious freedom. Reading the text of the RFRA is a good place to start. I include Section 2 here:

SECTION 2. CONGRESSIONAL FINDINGS AND DECLARATION OF PURPOSES.

1. Findings. The Congress finds that
   (a) the framers of the Constitution, recognizing free exercise of religion as an unalienable right, secured its protection in the First Amendment to the Constitution;
   (b) laws "neutral" toward religion may burden religious exercise as surely as laws intended to interfere with religious exercise;

    (c) governments should not substantially burden religious exercise
without compelling justification;

    (d) in Employment Division v. Smith, 494 U.S. 872 (1990) the
Supreme Court virtually eliminated the requirement that the
government justify burdens on religious exercise imposed by
laws neutral toward religion; and

    (e) the compelling interest test as set forth in prior Federal court
rulings is a workable test for striking sensible balances between
religious liberty and competing prior governmental interests.

2. Purposes. The purposes of this Act are

    (a) to restore the compelling interest test as set forth in Sherbert v.
Verner, 374 U.S. 398 (1963) and Wisconsin v. Yoder, 406
U.S. 205 (1972) and to guarantee its application in all cases
where free exercise of religion is substantially burdened; and

    (b) to provide a claim or defense to persons whose religious exer-
cise is substantially burdened by government.[16]

In Section 2 (b)(1), Congress makes a mistake in attempting to over-
ride the Court by legislating how laws, in particular *Sherbert v. Verner* and
Wisconsin v. Yoder, should be understood and applied. It doesn't matter
what *Sherbert* and *Wisconsin* are about, what matters is whether Congress
should enact legislation that orders the Supreme Court on how it should
adjudicate cases. Why would Congress need to pass legislation that reiter-
ates law as it was already largely understood? Politics. In Section 2 (a)(2),
Congress states that neutral laws may burden religious exercise, and that
is true; but could one also make a legitimate claim that a state should not
criminalize dangerous drug use? Can a state make an argument that crimi-
nalizing dangerous drugs is a compelling justification for negatively
impacting the exercise of religious practices that include the use of dangerous drugs? In Section 2 (a)(4), Congress states that in *Employment
Division v. Smith* "the Supreme Court virtually eliminated the requirement that the government justify burdens on religious exercise imposed
by laws neutral toward religion." Did it? Our branches of government
engage in power struggles over religion and law. This particular power
struggle was resolved in *City of Boerne v. P. F. Flores, Archbishop of San
Antonio, and U.S.*, where the Court found that the Religious Freedom
Restoration Act exceeded Congress's power.

In *Boerne v. Flores*, the archbishop of San Antonio, Texas, wanted to accommodate more parishioners by enlarging his church building. Before renovations started, the Boerne City Council passed an ordinance that gave rights to the city's Historic Landmark Commission to preapprove construction projects, including the church in question. The Commission rejected the archbishop's application on historic preservation grounds and the city was sued on the basis of RFRA. It is not clear to me why the archbishop thought RFRA protected their church's desire to expand their building. Perhaps a reading of the Fifth Amendment is relevant here:

> No person shall be held to answer for a capital, or otherwise infamous crime, unless on a presentiment or indictment of a grand jury, except in cases arising in the land or naval forces, or in the militia, when in actual service in time of war or public danger; nor shall any person be subject for the same offense to be twice put in jeopardy of life or limb; nor shall be compelled in any criminal case to be a witness against himself, nor be deprived of life, liberty, or property, without due process of law; nor shall private property be taken for public use, without just compensation.[17]

The archbishop may have felt that his church's property rights were being violated, but, suspecting that he could not win on a Fifth Amendment violation, he chose to pursue a religious freedom claim. Nevertheless, after a lengthy history lesson, the Court said, "We now turn to consider whether RFRA can be considered enforcement legislation under Section 5 of the Fourteenth Amendment."[18]

The Fourteenth Amendment, Section 1, states,

> Section 1.
> All persons born or naturalized in the United States, and subject to the jurisdiction thereof, are citizens of the United States and of the state wherein they reside. No state shall make or enforce any law which shall abridge the privileges or immunities of citizens of the United States; nor shall any state deprive any person of life, liberty, or property, without due process of law; nor deny to any person within its jurisdiction the equal protection of the laws.[19]

Did the archbishop believe his community was being deprived of property based on religious discrimination? Did he believe the city of Boerne's interest in historic preservation should not have superseded the church's interest in expanding property for religious practice? Their argument is not expressly stated in the opinion, but deductive reasoning suggests that the archbishop believed the US Supreme Court would require the city of Boerne to allow their expansion on religious freedom grounds. The Court decided that RFRA

> cannot be considered remedial, preventive legislation. ... RFRA is so out of proportion to a supposed remedial or preventive object that it cannot be understood as responsive to, or designed to prevent, unconstitutional behavior. It appears, instead, to attempt a substantive change in constitutional protections.[20]

Furthermore, the Court said,

> Sweeping coverage ensures its intrusion at every level of government, displacing laws and prohibiting official actions of almost every description and regardless of subject matter. RFRA's restrictions apply to every agency and official of the Federal, State and local Governments. RFRA applies to all federal and state law, statutory or otherwise, whether adopted before or after its enactment. RFRA has no termination date or termination mechanism. Any law is subject to challenge at any time by any individual who alleges a substantial burden on his or her free exercise of religion.[21]

RFRA was found unconstitutional as federal law in 1997, so states decided to draft and adopt their own religious freedom statutes, including,

Alabama	Ala. Const. Art. I, §3.01
Arizona	Ariz. Rev. Stat. §41-1493.01
Arkansas	2015 SB 975, *enacted April 2, 2015*
Connecticut	Conn. Gen. Stat. §52-571b
Florida	Fla. Stat. §761.01, *et seq.*
Idaho	Idaho Code §73-402
Illinois	Ill. Rev. Stat. Ch. 775, §35/1, *et seq.*
Indiana	2015 SB 101, *enacted March 26, 2015;* 2015 SB 50, *enacted April 2, 2015*
Kansas	Kan. Stat. §60-5301, *et seq.*
Kentucky	Ky. Rev. Stat. §446.350
Louisiana	La. Rev. Stat. §13:5231, *et seq.*
Mississippi	Miss. Code §11-61-1
Missouri	Mo. Rev. Stat. §1.302
New Mexico	N.M. Stat. §28-22-1, *et seq.*
Oklahoma	Okla. Stat. tit. 51, §251, *et seq.*
Pennsylvania	Pa. Stat. tit. 71, §2403
Rhode Island	R.I. Gen. Laws §42-80.1-1, *et seq.*
South Carolina	S.C. Code §1-32-10, *et seq.*
Tennessee	Tenn. Code §4-1-407
Texas	Tex. Civ. Prac. & Remedies Code §110.001, *et seq.*
Virginia	Va. Code §57-2.02[22]

In 2017, nine states had religious freedom legislation pending, including,

Colorado	HB 1013	Concerns a person's free exercise of religion.
Georgia	SB 233	Relates to state government, to provide for the preservation of religious freedom. Provides for related matters. Provides for an effective date and applicability. Repeals conflicting laws.
Hawaii	HB 823	Prohibits the state or any county from burdening any person's right to exercise religion absent that burden being the least restrictive means of furthering a compelling governmental interest.
Kentucky	HB 105	Defines protected activities, protected activity provider, protected rights place of public accommodation, resort, or amusement, and standard goods or services. Provides legislative intent. Prohibits any statute, regulation, ordinance, order, judgment, of other law or action by any court, commission, or other public agency from impairing, impeding, infringing upon, or otherwise restricting the exercise of protected rights by any protected activity provider.
Mississippi	HB 1372	Provides for the Mississippi Religious Freedom Restoration Act. Provides for the Protecting Freedom of Conscience from Government Discrimination Act.
Oklahoma	SB 530	Relates to the Oklahoma Religious Freedom Act. Relates to definitions and burden upon free exercise of religion. Modifies definitions. Authorizes certain action. Authorizes certain relief. Provides an effective date.
Virginia	HB 791	Relates to the Act for Religious Freedom. Reaffirms that the religious rights asserted in a specified section of the Code are the natural and unalienable rights of mankind, and this declaration is the policy of the Commonwealth.
Washington	HB 1217	Concerns the burdening of exercises of religion and freedom of conscience.
West Virginia	SB 19	Creates West Virginia Freedom of Conscience Protection Act.[23]

In the absence of evidence that the federal government is establishing a religion, a religion to which we must belong, the proliferation of state religious freedom legislation must be understood in order to ensure the protection of minorities.

I began collecting data on spiritual caregivers and religious freedom when I lived in Georgia. At the time, I began reading about the varieties of religious freedom legislative efforts throughout the South and elsewhere, some of which targeted specific groups of unprotected US citizens within the LGBTQ communities who had found protection under the Obama administration and the Supreme Court marriage equality case

Obergefell v. Hodges. An example of a bill that targets specific groups and erodes protections is found in Indiana State bill signed by then-Governor Mike Pence in 2015. The bill reads in part:

Chapter 9. Religious Freedom Restoration

Sec. 7. As used in this chapter, "person" includes the following: (1) An individual. (2) An organization, a religious society, a church, a body of communicants, or a group organized and operated primarily for religious purposes. (3) A partnership, a limited liability company, a corporation, a company, a firm, a society, a joint-stock company, an unincorporated association, or another entity that: (A) may sue and be sued; and (B) exercises practices that are compelled or limited by a system of religious belief held by: (i) an individual; or (ii) the individuals; who have control and substantial ownership of the entity, regardless of whether the entity is organized and operated for profit or nonprofit purposes.

Sec. 8. (a) Except as provided in subsection (b), a governmental entity may not substantially burden a person's exercise of religion, SEA 101— Concur 3 even if the burden results from a rule of general applicability. (b) A governmental entity may substantially burden a person's exercise of religion only if the governmental entity demonstrates that application of the burden to the person: (1) is in furtherance of a compelling governmental interest; and (2) is the least restrictive means of furthering that compelling governmental interest.

Sec. 9. A person whose exercise of religion has been substantially burdened, or is likely to be substantially burdened, by a violation of this chapter may assert the violation or impending violation as a claim or defense in a judicial or administrative proceeding, regardless of whether the state or any other governmental entity is a party to the proceeding. If the relevant governmental entity is not a party to the proceeding, the governmental entity has an unconditional right to intervene in order to respond to the person's invocation of this chapter...

In Section 7 (3), the legislation seeks to bolster religious freedom rights for nonhuman persons, that is, partnerships, LLCs, and other types of companies. This legislative initiative, as well as similar initiatives throughout the United States, has been, in my view, legally pointless, unwise, and costly. Human rights advocates argued that Indiana SB 101 was an attempt to undermine equal protection under existing law. Human rights activists argued that SB 101 would cost Indiana millions of dollars. Some even threatened to leave the state, forcing then-Governor Pence to sign Senate Enrolled Act No. 50, an amendment to SB 101, which reads in part,

SECTION1.IC34-13-9-0.7 IS ADDED TO THE INDIANA CODE AS A NEW SECTION TO READ AS FOLLOWS [EFFECTIVE JULY 1, 2015]: Sec. 0.7. This chapter does not: (1) authorize a provider to refuse to offer or provide services, facilities, use of public accommodations, goods, employment, or housing to any member or members of the general public on the basis of race, color, religion, ancestry, age, national origin, disability, sex, sexual orientation, gender identity, or United States military service; (2) establish a defense to a civil action or criminal prosecution for refusal by a provider to offer or provide services, facilities, use of public accommodations, goods, employment, or housing to any member or members of the general public on the basis of race, color, religion, ancestry, age, national origin, disability, sex, sexual orientation, gender identity, or United States military service; or (3) negate any rights available under the Constitution of the State of Indiana.[24]

Indiana's RFRA legislative fiasco and opposition was felt in Georgia when Georgia attempted to promulgate and pass its own RFRA:

The fallout from these bills went far beyond employer opposition to include significant economic harm to state economies. After the Indiana General Assembly passed the first overly broad version of the state RFRA, the Center for American Progress found that the measure lost or put at-risk more than $250 million from Indiana's economy. Despite a subsequent rollback of the RFRA's scope, the state still "may have lost as much as $60 million in hotel profits, tax revenue and other economic benefits" due to the law's passage. In Georgia, which is currently considering its own discriminatory RFRA, two leading business groups have estimated that passage of the legislation could cost the Atlanta region between $1 billion and $2 billion in economic activity.[25]

Governor Nathan Deal, to protect Georgia's economy, vetoed the Georgia bill.

As a spiritual caregiver with a legal education, I wondered what my pastoral and spiritual care peers and colleagues thought about this growth of state legislative activities around the religious freedom to discriminate,[26] especially as I predicted Trump would become president. With this frenzy of legislation to "restore" religious freedom, one might ask, had religious freedom to believe whatever one wants to believe, been taken away? Had religious freedom to practice or enact those beliefs on others been eroded?

The data for this book includes a 2017 survey of chaplains in the South. Forty-three chaplains throughout the South participated in the "Religious

Freedom for Chaplains" survey. Forty-six percent said they were unfamiliar with the Religious Freedom Restoration Act of 1993, 19 percent said they were familiar, and 35 percent said they were somewhat familiar. The numbers were about the same for their state's religious freedom laws. Sixty-five percent of respondents worked in hospitals. None had ever provided expert advice to lawmakers drafting their state's religious freedom laws. Eighty-eight percent had not lobbied against their state's religious freedom law, 7 percent had lobbied against the law, 2 percent had lobbied for a version of the law that explicitly identified a group of people, and 2 percent had lobbied for a version of the law that did not explicitly identify a group of people.

In the "Pastoral Counselors Religious Freedom Pre-Survey," to which 34 pastoral counselors in the South responded, 35 percent said they were unfamiliar with the federal Religious Freedom Restoration Act of 1993, 6 percent said they were familiar, and 47 percent said they were somewhat familiar. Forty-four percent said they were unfamiliar with the state's religious freedom law, 15 percent said they were familiar, and 41 percent said they were somewhat familiar. Ninety-seven percent said they had not provided expert advice to lawmakers drafting their state's religious freedom law, 82 percent said they had not lobbied for or against the law, but 18 percent said they had lobbied against the law. In the 2018 survey "Chaplain Educators and Religious Freedom Curriculum" 65 percent of chaplain educators said they were aware of the rights in RFRA 1993, and 35 percent said they were not, yet 78 percent said they did not educate their interns and residents about RFRA 1993. As it relates to the First Amendment, 100 percent of chaplain educators said they were aware of the rights in the First Amendment, but 69 percent said they did not educate their residents and interns about it. Seventy-five percent of chaplain educators did not educate their students about the Fourteenth Amendment equal protection clause. They should. On May 4, 2017, President Trump signed this religious liberty executive order. The order reads, in part:

> ...Section 1. Policy. It shall be the policy of the executive branch to vigorously enforce Federal law's robust protections for religious freedom...The executive branch will honor and enforce those protections.
>
> Sec. 2. Respecting Religious and Political Speech. All executive departments and agencies (agencies) shall, to the greatest extent practicable and to the extent permitted by law, respect and protect the freedom of persons and organizations to engage in religious and political speech. In particular, the

Secretary of the Treasury shall ensure, to the extent permitted by law, that the Department of the Treasury does not take any adverse action against any individual, house of worship, or other religious organization on the basis that such individual or organization speaks or has spoken about moral or political issues from a religious perspective, where speech of similar character has, consistent with law, not ordinarily been treated as participation or intervention in a political campaign on behalf of (or in opposition to) a candidate for public office by the Department of the Treasury...

Sec. 4. Religious Liberty Guidance. In order to guide all agencies in complying with relevant Federal law, the Attorney General shall, as appropriate, issue guidance interpreting religious liberty protections in Federal law...[27]

What former Indiana Governor Pence attempted and failed to accomplish in Indiana in 2015 is what he helped put in place as vice president of the United States, affecting all 50 states. On its face, the executive order seems constitutional and consistent with the national value of religious liberty, but it does not promote *responsible* religious liberty. It does not reiterate that the judiciary has the right to find religious practices unconstitutional if there is a compelling state or governmental interest to do so, or even find the religious practices criminal if religious liberty exercises result in harming others. A compelling governmental interest test is the way the Court determines, in religious freedom cases, whether a law is constitutional. The test attempts to balance the government's interests and individual interests and theoretically will uphold the government's interests only if they are compelling, and where the means to achieve the goal is the least restrictive means.[28]

It is important for US citizens to understand that the government can interfere with religious practice when the practice of one's religion infringes upon another's constitutionally protected rights. Concerning respecting religious and political speech, this executive order, on its face, seems to affirm values we already hold, but it signals that religious speech in politics will be met with more liberty than in the past. In other words, one's religious speech should have the weight of political power in the public domain, but is the conventional understanding of speech (talking, signing, writing) the same as religious practice? Trump's speech is code for saying cases like *Roe v. Wade*, a case about religious beliefs and about the sanctity of life from conception colliding with the need for women to exercise agency over their bodies, is still at issue and in play. The secretary of Health and Human Services (HHS) not only has considered issuing amended regulations consistent with this order, but two days after President Trump's Religious Freedom Day speech, HHS actually created an enforcement mechanism per this executive order. Trump said,

> Today, Americans from diverse ethnic and religious backgrounds remain steadfast in a commitment to the inherent values of faith, honesty, integrity, and patriotism. Our Constitution and laws guarantee Americans the right not just to believe as they see fit, but to freely exercise their religion. Unfortunately, not all have recognized the importance of religious freedom, whether by threatening tax consequences for particular forms of religious speech, or forcing people to comply with laws that violate their core religious beliefs without sufficient justification. These incursions, little by little, can destroy the fundamental freedom underlying our democracy. Therefore, soon after taking office, I addressed these issues in an Executive Order that helps ensure Americans are able to follow their consciences without undue Government interference and the Department of Justice has issued guidance to Federal agencies regarding their compliance with laws that protect religious freedom. No American—whether a nun, nurse, baker, or business owner—should be forced to choose between the tenets of faith or adherence to the law.

The democratic rule of law is equal protection. The "rule" of Christian "law" is caring for the vulnerable. These are mutually supporting principles. According to Sullivan, "Christians, laypersons as well as clergy, like many others, regard visiting the sick and those otherwise disadvantaged, to be a religious obligation."[29] In Trump's speech, he signals to those listening that his administration's attempt to broaden religious freedom is not just about speech, but also about other religious practices. He does not mention that not every religious practice is constitutional or runs the risk of being found unconstitutional for compelling state reasons; instead, he uses the phrase "sufficient justification." "Sufficient justification" is not a constitutional standard, but perhaps this is a signal that he believes some members of federal courts and the Supreme Court should lower the standard from compelling governmental interest to "sufficient justification," or compelling governmental interest should be interpreted as "sufficient justification."

Can the Executive office put pressure on the judicial branch, as President Trump has attempted to do, by taunting and accusing judges of being politically motivated? Perhaps anticipating a favorable decision from the Supreme Court on the 2018 *Masterpiece Cakeshop v. Colorado Civil Rights*

Commission case, Trump ends his speech saying that nuns (some of whom have objected to contraceptives), nurses, a baker, or a business owner should not be forced to choose between their religion or law. In other words, arguably, Trump does not respect the rule of law as it relates to religious practice as the justices in *Reynolds* did. Has the Trump presidency become the era for religious anarchy?

Two days after Trump's Religious Freedom Day speech, the HHS issued this press release:

> HHS Announces New Conscience and Religious Freedom Division
> Today, the U.S. Department of Health and Human Services (HHS) is pleased to announce the formation of a new Conscience and Religious Freedom Division in the HHS Office for Civil Rights (OCR)...
> The Conscience and Religious Freedom Division has been established to restore federal enforcement of our nation's laws that protect the fundamental and unalienable rights of conscience and religious freedom. OCR is the law enforcement agency within HHS that enforces federal laws protecting civil rights and conscience in health and human services, and the security and privacy of people's health information. The creation of the new division will provide HHS with the focus it needs to more vigorously and effectively enforce existing laws protecting the rights of conscience and religious freedom, the first freedom protected in the Bill of Rights...
> OCR Director Roger Severino said, "Laws protecting religious freedom and conscience rights are just empty words on paper if they aren't enforced. No one should be forced to choose between helping sick people and living by one's deepest moral or religious convictions, and the new division will help guarantee that victims of unlawful discrimination find justice. For too long, governments big and small have treated conscience claims with hostility instead of protection, but change is coming and it begins here and now."[30]

Regarding this Health and Human Services announcement, the *Washington Post* reported,

> A new civil rights division within the Department of Health and Human Services will protect health care workers who refuse to provide services that run counter to their moral or religious convictions, the Trump administration announced Thursday.
> This office will consider complaints from doctors, nurses and others who feel they have been pressured by employers to "perform, accommodate or assist with" procedures that violate their beliefs. If a complaint about coercion or retribution is found to be valid, an *entity receiving federal dollars could have that funding revoked* [italics mine].[31]

Typically, in cases of workplace discrimination, entire organizations are not at risk of closing. The Conscience and Religious Freedom Division of the Office for Civil Rights is an extreme attempt to appease political supporters while putting poorer and middle-class supporters at risk of losing valuable health care access. It is true that in the United States, the government should not police ordinary people, forcing them to be Good Samaritans while in their homes or walking down a private path, but the deepest moral and religious convictions in this country move people toward Good Samaritan behavior. How will CRFD enforcement impact chaplains? Sullivan says,

> Recent shifts in interpretation of the religion clauses that suggest a greater tolerance on the part of the Supreme Court toward government funding of religious entities have been accompanied by the always present proviso that there are core activities that the establishment clause prohibits government from directly funding or sponsoring, that is, worship and proselytizing. ... And yet, notwithstanding these apparently obvious constitutional difficulties with having ministers hired by and working for the government, there is relatively little law about the constitutionality of government-run chaplaincies.[32]

It is not yet known what the impact on chaplains is or will be, but Office for Civil Rights enforcement with the threat of a loss of funding for an entire health care organization is a challenge to the universalizing spirituality and neutral religious exercise for which chaplains are known and loved. The OCR online complaint form states and asks,

> If you believe that a covered entity discriminated against you or violated your (or someone else's) conscience or religious freedom, you may file a complaint with the Office for Civil Rights (OCR). Federal conscience and religious freedom laws protect you from coercion, discrimination on the basis of conscience or religion, and burdens on the free exercise of religion.

The following are some examples of potential covered entities (including institutions and personnel) that must abide by federal conscience and religious freedom laws:

- State and local government agencies that are responsible for administering health care
- State and local government income assistance and human service agencies

- Hospitals
- Medicaid and Medicare providers
- Physicians and other health care professionals in private practice with patients assisted by Medicaid
- Family health centers
- Community mental health centers
- Alcohol and drug treatment centers
- Nursing homes
- Foster care homes
- Public and private adoption and foster care agencies
- Day care centers
- Senior citizen centers
- Nutrition programs
- Any entity established under the Affordable Care Act
- Health insurance plans or companies
- HMOs
- Pharmacies
- Homeless shelters
- Health researchers[33]

According to "Fierce Healthcare," as of February 20, 2018, 300 complaints had been filed by health care workers.[34] That is 300 complaints in less than one month. In August 2018, I twice attempted to submit my first Freedom of Information Act request regarding CRFD with Health and Human Services. They replied that they received the request, but they never fulfilled the request. The HHS press release stating, "No one should be forced to choose between helping sick people and living by one's deepest moral or religious convictions," brings to mind another constitutional standard: the reasonable person standard. Is it reasonable to craft and issue a policy that gives health care employees the right not to help sick people when they work for a health care organization? According to Legal Dictionary, an online resource, "reasonable person" is defined as

A phrase frequently used in tort and criminal law to denote a hypothetical person in society who exercises average care, skill, and judgment in conduct and who serves as a comparative standard for determining liability. The decision whether an accused is guilty of a given offense might involve the application of an objective text in which the conduct of the accused is compared to that of a reasonable person under similar circumstances. In most cases, persons with greater than average skills, or with special duties to society, are held to a higher standard of care. For example, a physician who aids a person in distress is held to a higher standard of care than is an ordinary person.[35]

Despite Trump's executive order and the Department of Health and Human Services enforcement mechanism, a nurse, reasonably, should still be held to a higher standard of care, especially while in the act of nursing. A baker, reasonably, should not be held to such a standard. Executive orders and enforcement mechanisms that promote medical malpractice should be found unconstitutional, because there is a compelling state governmental interest in protecting citizens' safety and health, and protecting the quality of health care citizens receive. Laws and policies that promote malpractice are also unethical. The US culture promotes Good Samaritan acts of compassion, service, and courage when newscasters portray acts of heroism and when health care organizations are named "Good Samaritan" or "Samaritan." President Trump's executive order and Health and Human Services' CRFD enforcement mechanism promote a warped version of Christianity and also promote medical malpractice by discrimination and neglect. About six months after Health and Human Services announced the creation of the CRFD enforcement arm, the Supreme Court ruled on a case that had started in 2012—the widely misunderstood "Gay Cake Case."

THE NO-BAKING-WEDDING-CAKES-FOR-GAYS CASE

On June 4, 2018, The Supreme Court ruled in favor of a Colorado cake baker who refused to bake a wedding cake for a same-sex couple. The ruling was lauded by some as a victory for the religious freedom to discriminate against gay people and, by extension, all members of the LGBTQ community. Although the case, *Masterpiece Cakeshop v. Colorado Civil Rights Commission*, represents a victory for religious freedom and a defeat for gay rights, it is not in actuality a legal victory for the religious freedom to discriminate against "sexual minorities," and it is not a defeat of gay rights. The case should not be taken by health care workers, including pastoral and spiritual caregivers and chaplains, to mean that they can discriminate against transgender hospital patients, or any patient, based on their religious beliefs. The Court actually concludes that the Colorado Civil Rights Commission, a state governmental entity, was comprised of members who were hostile toward the cake baker's religious convictions, and therefore the baker did not have a fair hearing. Were the Colorado Civil Rights commissioners actually hostile toward the baker's religious beliefs?

Justice Anthony Kennedy wrote the majority opinion, with Justices John Roberts, Samuel Alito, Elena Kagan, and Neil Gorsuch concurring. Justice Kagan wrote a separate concurring opinion with Justice Stephen Breyer concurring. Justice Gorsuch wrote his own concurring opinion with Alito concurring, Justice Clarence Thomas wrote his own concurring opinion with Gorsuch concurring, and Justice Ruth Bader Ginsberg wrote the dissenting opinion with Sonia Sotomayor concurring. Kennedy, Roberts, Alito, Kagan, Gorsuch, Breyer, and Thomas all agreed that the Colorado Civil Rights Commission was hostile toward the baker's religious beliefs. Kennedy, for the court, wrote,

> On July 25, 2014, the Commission met again. This meeting, too, was conducted in public and on the record. On this occasion another commissioner made specific reference to the previous meeting's discussion but said far more to disparage Phillips' beliefs. The commissioner stated: "I would also like to reiterate what we said in the hearing or the last meeting. Freedom of religion and religion has been used to justify all kinds of discrimination through history, whether it be slavery, whether it be the holocaust, whether it be—I mean, we—we can list hundreds of situations where freedom of religion has been used to justify discrimination. And to me it is one of the most despicable pieces of rhetoric that people can use to—to use their religion to hurt others."[36]

Compare the commissioner's statement to this unrelated but informative quotation from Vietnamese Zen Master Thich Nhat Hanh, a proponent of religions and Buddhist-Christian interreligious dialogue:

> There are many people who in the name of faith or love persecute countless people around them. If I believe that my notion about God, about happiness, about nirvana is perfect, I want very much to impose that notion on you. I will say that if you don't believe as I do, you will not be happy. I will do everything I can to impose my notions on you, and therefore I will destroy you. I will make you unhappy for the whole of your life.[37]

If the commissioner's statement is hostile toward religion, then Nhat Hanh's statement is as well, but those who know Zen Buddhist priest Nhat Hanh and his advocacy for Buddhist-Christian dialogue, know he is an advocate for religion, not hostile toward it. The commissioner's statement may have been misinterpreted; nevertheless, Kennedy continues,

> To describe a man's faith as "one of the most despicable pieces of rhetoric that people can use" is to disparage his religion in at least two distinct ways; by describing it as despicable, and also by characterizing it as merely rhetorical—something insubstantial and even insincere. The commissioner even went so far as to compare Phillips' invocation of his sincerely held religious beliefs to defenses of slavery and the Holocaust."[38]

When did "sincerely held belief" become the standard for determining whether a belief is actually a *religious* belief? Did the commissioner, a member of the Colorado Civil Rights Commission, created to protect civil and human rights, actually describe Christianity in this way? Was the commissioner talking about the ways people use religion to treat people inhumanely? Is religion itself rhetoric or has religion been used rhetorically to justify dehumanizing others? I agree with a statement in Justice Thomas's separate concurring opinion. He says, "This Court is not an authority on matters of conscience, and its decisions can (and often should) be criticized."[39]

My analysis and critique of *Masterpiece Cakeshop v. Colorado Civil Rights Commission* follows. Justice Kennedy is partially correct in saying,

> The case presents difficult questions as to the proper reconciliation of at least two principles. The first is the authority of a State and its governmental entities to protect the rights and dignity of gay persons who are, or wish to be, married but who face discrimination when they seek goods or services. The second is the right of all persons to exercise fundamental freedoms under the First Amendment, as applied to the States through the Fourteenth Amendment.[40]

Kennedy is partially correct in that there are opposing constitutional principles that are difficult to reconcile, but he does not choose the proper pair of constitutional principles to reconcile. On one side, he chooses a same-sex couple that wants to marry and should not be discriminated against; on the other side lies the right of a business owner to exercise fundamental freedoms under the First and Fourteenth Amendments. The problem with this characterization of the dialectic is, on one side, marriage equality is not even an issue in the case. Same-sex marriage was not legal in Colorado and Jack Phillips, the baker, did not sue the commission regarding marriage equality. On the other side, secular business owners do not have the right to discriminate against potential customers based on their religious beliefs. Kennedy set up a false dialectic, which perhaps gave birth to a cascade of separate concurring opinions.

The more appropriate characterization of the principles in need of reconciliation are, on one side, can someone who wants to buy a wedding cake from a bakery that is open to the public legally be refused that particular service due to the customer's private purposes for buying the cake, in this case, to celebrate a wedding? On the other side, should a baker, who is aware of the intended purpose of the cake, be compelled to bake it, when, based on his religion, he believes the customer is a sinner? When a US citizen walks into a business that is open to the public, should they expect they are potentially walking into a house of worship? Should a secular business owner, who operates a business as a ministry, return their secular business license and apply for a religious organization permit? When does religious freedom to believe what one wants to believe become a constitutionally protected right to practice whatever one wants to practice even if that practice falls outside the norm of a religious community's practice? For example, Phillips claimed baking wedding cakes is a religious practice for him. Most Christians do not bake wedding cakes. There is no tradition of baking wedding cakes in the New Testament, Christian seminarians are not taught to bake wedding cakes, and wedding cakes are not considered sacramental items. What is the standard for determining what is religious practice when one's religious rights negatively impact another's equal protection rights? The phrase "sincerely held belief" is a red herring, seemingly legitimate but superficial as it relates to religion, spirituality, and theology. "Sincerely held belief," like Trump's "sufficient justification," serves to distract from actual standards, relevant facts, and the subject at hand: What is a legitimate religious practice that overrides another citizen's equal protection rights?

When the Fourteenth Amendment right to equal protection for all US citizens is pitted against the First Amendment right to practice an individual's religion, how is that to be resolved by the Supreme Court? Phillips sued the Colorado Civil Rights Commission; therefore the Court had to determine the facts presented by these entities.

Here are some key facts: One man, planning to wed a man outside Colorado because neither Colorado nor the United States at that time had legalized same-sex marriage, walked into Masterpiece Cakeshop to buy a wedding cake. The baker refused to bake the cake and offered him the privilege of buying other items from his bakery. The couple took their complaint to the Colorado Civil Rights Commission (CCRC), which adjudicates complaints brought under the Colorado Anti-Discrimination Act (CADA). The act reads in part,

> It is a discriminatory practice and unlawful for a person, directly or indirectly, to refuse, withhold from, or deny to an individual or a group, because of disability, race, creed, color, sex, sexual orientation, marital status, national origin, or ancestry, the full and equal engagement of the goods, services, facilities, privileges, advantages, or accommodations of a place of public accommodation.

The CADA was amended in 2007 and 2008 to protect against discrimination based on sexual orientation.[41] On its face, it seems clear that CADA prohibits discrimination based on sexual orientation, but CADA alone does not address whether or not a Colorado citizen can invoke their right to religious freedom under the First Amendment in order to discriminate. The Colorado Division of Civil Rights found probable cause for a CADA violation and the case was referred to the CCRC. The CCRC referred the case to an administrative law judge who ruled for the couple. The CCRC and the Colorado Court of Appeals affirmed the administrative law judge's decision without answering the question of whether or not the baker had a right to exercise his religion by refusing to bake a wedding cake for a gay customer. The Supreme Court, despite the political rhetoric around the case, also has neither answered that question nor resolved the dialectical tensions in the case. Instead, the Court decided that some of the commissioners expressed hostility toward the baker's religious beliefs and that commissioners, when deciding on religious freedom cases, need to adopt a standard of neutrality. Kennedy, for the majority, wrote,

> The Commission gave "every appearance," of adjudicating his religious objection based on a negative normative "evaluation of the particular justification" for his objection and the religious grounds for it, but government has no role in expressing or even suggesting whether the religious ground for Phillips' conscience-based objection is legitimate or illegitimate. The inference here is thus that Phillips' religious objection was not considered with the neutrality required by the Free Exercise Clause. The State's interest could have been weighted against Phillips' sincere religious objections in a way consistent with the requisite religious neutrality that must be strictly observed. But the official expressions of hostility to religion in some of the

commissioners' comments were inconsistent with that requirement, and the Commission's disparate consideration of Phillips' case compared to the cases of the other bakers suggests the same.[42]

The Supreme Court did not decide that Phillips has the right to discriminate against gay people; the Court also did not decide that the couple, Charlie Craig and Dave Mullins, have the right to buy a wedding cake from Phillips. The Court found that some of the commissioners, as government agents, were hostile toward Phillips's beliefs and did not give him a religiously neutral hearing. The Court did not decide whether there was a compelling governmental interest to find Phillips's practices, in the name of religion, unconstitutional. The majority opinion gives little to no guidance on the connection between Phillips's religious belief (that same-sex couples should not have the right to marry, a belief shared by many Christians), freedom of speech (not at issue), and exercise of the belief (refusing products and services). But what if the belief was expressed through a sign in the window stating, "We do not bake wedding cakes for gay couples?" What if the exercise of the belief was to engage in the ancient religious practice of stoning sinners?

Constitutional questions remain unsettled and will always remain unsettled when constitutional rights are in opposition and the government has no compelling interest to deny those rights. Chaplain educators, chaplains, and pastoral caregivers in hospital settings have choices to make with respect to the transgender patients who enter their hospitals. They can become better educated about the First and Fourteenth Amendments, the federal Religious Freedom Restoration Act, state religious freedom laws, the Department of Health and Human Services Office for Civil Rights Conscience and Religious Freedom Division, and Supreme Court case law. Alternatively, instead of becoming more law-literate, we can simply continue listening to the political rhetoric around religious freedom and hence deepen our confusion about what is legally appropriate. We can follow the norms of our religious communities, we can contemplate our professional codes of ethics, and we can engage in interreligious dialogue. We can also become more religious-freedom-law literate and advocate on behalf of legally targeted trans citizens. There are already signs of a commitment to do so.

In the previously mentioned 2018 survey, chaplain educators reported that they would help their students decide how to make care decisions by utilizing the following:

Professional standards of care (21 percent)
Chaplaincy organization's professional code of ethics (20 percent)
Hospital professional expectations (20 percent)
The interns' or residents' own religious traditions and practices (18 percent)
The interns' or residents' own values (12 percent)
The U.S. Constitution (7 percent)
Other (2 percent)

The "other" category includes, "Taking the family/patient's beliefs into account," "The value of respecting others," and "Religious instructions to love others, self-awareness, and understanding/respecting others." These data suggest that we need to increase US Constitutional literacy.

There is no true separation between church and state, and the United States has not established a religion. However, the Trump-Pence administration has created a political situation, the courts have created legal situations, and federal and state legislation have contributed to political and legal situations whereby US citizens feel they have the religious freedom to *prey* (pun intended) on politically vulnerable transgender Americans, even when they are patients in hospitals. If chaplains are to continue to embody Good Samaritan qualities of character and ethical behavior, they will benefit by learning more about law and by thinking like a lawyer, especially the lawyer in The Parable of the Good Samaritan. Shifting the paradigm from chaplain as the loving and compassionate bed-side spiritual companion, to chaplain as liberative oriented theologians re-interpreting The Parable of the Good Samaritan beyond one-on-one care, spiritual caregivers can offer communal spiritual care consistent with constitutional rights and protections. Re-imagining and expanding spiritual care paradigms will allow spiritual caregivers in hospitals to shock their hospital systems back into radical hospitality and cohabitation for trans patients.

NOTES

1. Pichette, Aurora Jade, "Passing Through Divinity: An Anti-Oppressive Window into Trans Women and Religion," Ryerson University, MSW, Toronto, ON, Canada, 2013.
2. Pichette, 33.
3. Ibid., 35.
4. Sullivan, 97.

5. How Many Adults Identify as Transgender in the United States. https://williamsinstitute.law.ucla.edu/research/how-many-adults-identify-as-transgender-in-the-united-states/ (Accessed September 12, 2018).
6. Winnifred Fallers Sullivan, *A Ministry of Presence: Chaplaincy, Spiritual Care, and the Law* (Chicago: University of Chicago Press, 2014), xi.
7. Sullivan, 115.
8. www.justia, *Katcoff v. Marsh*, 582 F. Supp. 463 (E.D.N.Y. 1984), 4.
9. Ibid., 6.
10. Ibid., 17.
11. Ibid., 18.
12. Ibid., 21.
13. Employment Division, Department of Human Resources of Oregon, et. al. v. Alfred L. Smith et. al. 110 S.Ct. 2605 (1990).
14. Ibid., 1600.
15. Ibid.
16. Congress.gov https://www.congress.gov/bill/103rd-congress/house-bill/1308/text (Accessed October 3, 2018).
17. Cornell Law School https://www.law.cornell.edu/constitution/fifth_amendment (Accessed October 5, 2018).
18. City of Boerne, Petitioner v. P.F. Flores, Archbishop of San Antonio, and United States, 521 U.S. _____ (1997), 19.
19. Cornell Law School https://www.law.cornell.edu/constitution/amend-mentxiv (Accessed October 3, 2018).
20. Boerne v. Flores, 22.
21. Ibid., 23.
22. STATE RELIGIOUS FREEDOM RESTORATION ACTS http://www.ncsl.org/research/civil-and-criminal-justice/state-rfra-statutes.aspx (Accessed September 12, 2018).
23. 2017 Religious Freedom Restoration Act http://www.ncsl.org/research/civil-and-criminal-justice/2017-religious-freedom-restoration-act-legislation.aspx (Accessed September 12, 2018).
24. Senate Enrolled Act No. 50 http://iga.in.gov/static-documents/2/0/b/9/20b9d495/SB0050.08.ENRH.pdf (Accessed August 12, 2019).
25. The Economic Cost of Overly Broad RFRAs https://www.americanprogress.org/issues/lgbt/news/2016/02/04/130566/the-economic-cost-of-overly-broad-rfras/ (Accessed September 12, 2018).
26. 2017 Religious Freedom Restoration Act Legislation http://www.ncsl.org/research/civil-and-criminal-justice/2017-religious-freedom-restoration-act-legislation.aspx (Accessed September 12, 2018).
27. https://www.whitehouse.gov/presidential-actions/president-donald-j-trump-proclaims-january-16-2018-religious-freedom-day/ (Accessed September 3, 2018).

28. https://definitions.uslegal.com/c/compelling-state-interest-test/ (Accessed September 3, 2018).
29. Sullivan, 123.
30. https://www.hhs.gov/about/news/2018/01/18/hhs-ocr-announces-new-conscience-and-religious-freedom-division.html (Accessed September 3, 2018).
31. https://www.washingtonpost.com/news/to-your-health/wp/2018/01/18/new-hhs-civil-rights-division-charged-with-protecting-health-workers-with-moral-objections/?utm_term=.c0deebc82b0f (Accessed July 10, 2018).
32. Sullivan, 149.
33. U.S. Department of Health & Human Services Office for Civil Rights Complaint Portal Assistant https://ocrportal.hhs.gov/ocr/smartscreen/main.jsf (Accessed February 27, 2019).
34. Finnegan, Joanne, "New HHS office that protects religious rights has received more than 300 complaints from health workers," Fierce Health Care, February 22, 2018 https://www.fiercehealthcare.com/practices/more-than-300-complaints-health-workers-hhs-religious-rights-donald-trump (Accessed January 11, 2018).
35. https://legal-dictionary.thefreedictionary.com/Reasonable+person+standard (Accessed September 3, 2018).
36. Masterpiece Cakeshop, Ltd., et al., v. Colorado Civil Rights Commission et al., 584 US. _____(2018), 13.
37. Nhat Hanh, *Going Home: Jesus and Buddha as Brothers*, Riverhead Books, 1997, 80.
38. Ibid., 13.
39. Opinion of Thomas, J., 14.
40. Masterpiece Cakeshop, 2.
41. Ibid., 5.
42. Ibid., 3.

CHAPTER 5

A New "Shock Method" for Creating a Compassionate Health Care Team

Abstract Health care organizations receiving federal funds have been threatened by the Trump-Pence efforts to enforce the religious freedom to discriminate. African-American queer dharma leaders Rev. angel Kyodo Williams, Lama Rod Owens, and Professor Jasmine Syedullah, authors of *Radical Dharma: Talking Race, Love, and Liberation,* and White Christian theologian Brita Gill-Austern's teachings on practical solidarity are combined to produce methods for hate-proofing hospitals, shocking the system out of fear of governmental reprisals for promoting radical love and compassion for transgender patients.

Keywords Angel Kyodo Williams • Bodhisattva • Brita Gill-Austern • Jasmine Syedullah • Lama Rod Owens • Shantideva • Solidarity

When I was first involved in the religion with my first godfather, it was determined by divination that I needed to become a priest. So, I got together the money even though I was working minimum wage at the time, and I gave it to my godfather and we made all the preparations and about four weeks before we were supposed to go down to Florida to do my initiation, he called me on the phone and was like, "I have some bad news." And he was like, "Well, I spoke to the Oreate, the master of ceremonies, and he says that he refuses to initiate you as a woman." And this Oreate not only cancelled the ceremony when he found out I

was trans, he kept [$6,000]. I was devastated, and my godfather was
devastated, too. Thankfully, that worked out and I got initiated as a
woman and it went perfectly. The Orisha were totally happy.
(Pichette, 34)

Transgender people are under attack in virtually every sector of US society. Through the Executive Office, the Department of Health and Human Services Office for Civil Rights, and, arguably, through the Masterpiece Cake case, there has been a systematic attempt to "invisibilize" queer, LGBQI+, and trans people—a sort of legal and governmental systems technology of transcleansing that does not involve state-sanctioned murder, but attempts to sustain a culture and society that already contributes to a high rate of depression and suicide among and violence against transgender people. Hospitals (and other health care institutions), sites for transgender becoming and care, have been targeted as a ground zero for the reversal of trans people coming into fullness, wholeness, and enfranchisement. Chaplain educators (working with medical and social worker teams) stand in a unique, central, and morally powerful position to help create hate-proof zones within their hospitals.

Nearly all of the chaplain educators I surveyed said they had not filed a complaint of religious discrimination nor did they intend to do so, even in cases where an individual's religious tradition explicitly deemed certain groups of people as undeserving of spiritual care. When asked, "Who are the people your religion defines as less than or unworthy of receiving compassion from someone in your religious tradition?" options for responding included: agnostics, atheists, children, gay men, lesbians, men, non-Buddhists, non-Christians, people who have committed a crime, people with a sexually transmitted disease, anyone not a part of your religious tradition, transgender people, women, not applicable, other. Forty-four percent selected "not applicable." Six percent selected transgender people, gay men, and lesbians; 4 percent selected non-Christians, people who have committed a crime; and 2 percent selected agnostic, atheists, children, and women. Twenty percent of participants selected "other," but none qualified that choice in the blank space provided. Participants, however, did write in statements against discrimination, including, "My tradition values the dignity of each human person, so I would not say the tradition teaches not to have compassion for anyone," and, "All are included," and, "Everyone has God's mercy and deserves our love and compassionate presence."

There were significant religious and spiritual differences between chaplain educators and anti-transgender Christians the Trump-Pence administration purports to represent. This divide need not be played out solely on the backs of transgender patients. This divide can be resolved through interreligious dialogue, as discussed in Chap. 1, and can be met through systematic institutional change that can help prevent hospital systems from becoming victims of a Constitutional "chilling effect" for fear of governmental reprisals. Practicing freedom of speech, assembly, and religion all together is an act of resistance that can shock a system threatened with government closure. Is "shocking" the system necessary? Is shocking even congruent with notions of Buddhist compassion and Christian love? What is the bodhisattva ideal as it relates to seemingly intractable institutional change? Buddhists and non-Buddhists who embody the bodhisattva ideal of attending to others' suffering can effectuate institutional change especially by collaborating with others. But what, precisely, is the bodhisattva ideal?

In the Avatamsaka world, there are countless buddhas and bodhisattvas. One aspect of being a bodhisattva is emitting light. Nhat Hanh says,

> The first thing you notice is light, there's a lot of light. The beings that live in that realm that emit light, light, buddhas and bodhisattvas. Seems that everyone is a bodhisattva because there is always some amount of awakening of mindfulness in everyone. When you step into the realm of the Avatamsaka you [come in] contact [with] all these people, buddhas and bodhisattvas, all of them emit light from every pore of your body.[1]

For Nhat Hanh, a Buddhist community full of people practicing mindfulness, and thus the light of awareness, is living in the Avatamsaka realm. As a way of having retreatants imagine themselves as part of the Avatamsaka lineage of buddhas and bodhisattvas, Nhat Hanh says,

> [The] lion is an animal that has a very majestic way of walking and of sitting and lion seats are everywhere for you to enjoy sitting. In fact, in the Avatamsaka realm, every space, every spot you sit [in] becomes a lion seat because buddhas and bodhisattvas have sat already there several times in the past, so when you sit down on that very spot, you get the energy of a buddha or a bodhisattva.[2]

In the Avatamsaka world there are countless bodhisattvas, including Avalokiteshvara, who is a skilled listener, a result of mindfulness practice;[3]

Manjusri, who is the bodhisattva of deep looking;[4] and Samantabhadra, who is symbolized by a hand with an eye in the palm, because he is the bodhisattva of great action with insight.[5] These Mahayana Buddhist archetypal deities represent aspects of real persons on the path to enlightenment. Nhat Hanh says,

> These bodhisattvas are within yourself as seed.[6] You have the capacity of listening of looking deeply, of loving, but we have to train ourselves to touch the seed of these three things in us to help them to develop and then we'll be a person capable of loving, of bringing joy, and peace and reconciliation and stability to us and to the people we love.[7]

Nhat Hanh is a master at making the mythical and the archetypal real in the lives of real persons. Through mindfulness practices of deep touching, deep listening, and deep hearing, Nhat Hanh says one can transform the seeds of our unconscious minds. Deep touching, listening, and hearing should produce joyfulness, peace, and reconciliation. How, though, might we apply these practices to systematic institutional change?

Shantideva, an eighth-century Tibetan Buddhist monk, is credited with authoring instructions in the spiritual formation of real-life (not just archetypal) bodhisattvas. In *The Way of the Bodhisattva*[8] he outlines ways of transforming oneself from a person ruled by delusion, fear, and arrogance into one who lives for the awakening of others. Shantideva says,

> Bodhichitta, the awakening mind,
> In brief is said to have two aspects:
> First, aspiring, bodhichitta in intention;
> Then, active bodhichitta, practical engagement.[9]

On commitment, he writes,

> My body, thus, and all my goods besides,
> And all my merits gained and to be gained,
> I give them all away withholding nothing
> To bring about the benefit of beings.[10]

On vigilance,

> The hostile multitudes are vast as space—
> What chance is there that all should be subdued?

Let but this angry mind be overthrown
And every foe is then and there destroyed.[11]

And, on perseverance, he writes,

Heroic perseverance means delight in virtue.
Its contrary may be defined as laziness:
An inclination for unwholesome ways,
Despondency, and self-contempt.[12]

Though deeply touching seeds of compassion is helpful in the transformation of oneself, transforming "hostile multitudes" or institutional actors, takes more than self-transformation; it takes heroic perseverance, vigilance, commitment, and bodhichitta cultivation to change discriminating institutions.

The inspiration for an institutional shock method comes from African-American, queer, Buddhist practitioners Rev. angel Kyodo williams,[13] Lama Rod Owens, and Professor Jasmine Syedullah. Their consciousness-raising dialogues and encounters, their book *Radical Dharma: Talking Race, Love and Liberation,* and their subsequent Radical Dharma camp all contribute to ideas for institutional change. Finding that meditation, conventional dharma talks and writings on racism were not effectively creating more welcoming Buddhist communities in the United States, williams, Owens, and Syedullah began attempts at "shocking" predominately white sanghas, out of their entrenched racism. Their shock treatment included williams, Owens, and Syedullah joining forces and strategizing across lineages and schools (williams is a Soto Zen priest, Lama Rod Owens was trained in the Kagyu school of Tibetan Buddhism), partnering with sanghas outside their own schools (including Shambhala and Insight Meditation) and being in not-exclusively-Buddhist institutions including Harvard Divinity School and the Center for Transformative Change, founded by williams. They visited Atlanta, Georgia, Berkeley, California, Brooklyn, New York, and Cambridge, Massachusetts.[14]

The *Radical Dharma* shock method to transform racism was focused exclusively on American Buddhist communities, but this method may be adapted to other communities, like hospitals and hospices, and to other issues, like transphobia. When the resistance (bringing Berrigan and Nhat Hanh's Government Dialogue to mind) to hatred in a hospital lessens, and the rationale for the hatred becomes sublimated into intellectualism (a psychological defense) or religiosity, or some other collective defense mechanism, shocking the hospital into what it was founded to be, a place of hospitality and cohabitation, might be necessary in the interest of ensuring a civilized society, upholding the values of The Parable of the Good Samaritan, and our compelling governmental interests.

In a similar conceptual vein, medical professionals (and others) shock the arrested heart by using a defibrillator, and psychiatrists shock their drug- and therapy-resistant majorly depressed patients into psychological health through electroconvulsive therapy. Chaplains, working in collaboration with their departmental partners, as Dr. Rev. Gould, the social workers, and Dr. Seigel at Boston Medical Center have done, may need to shock the hearts and minds of their hospital culture. Chaplains and their partners will not use machines and medicine, but will use instead pastoral authority, ethical authenticity, relationality, compassion, solidarity, spiritual formation, and advocacy. This is not a quick fix. The cultivation of patience and determination, two character perfections shared by Buddhists and Christians, is required. Borrowing inspiration from *Radical Dharma*, I recommend:

- Chaplains should take time to become familiar with their own experiences (if any) in perpetuating religious discrimination. This reflection should include what their tradition teaches about what it means to be human and what it means to be favored by the God, gods, deities, prophets, founder, head teacher, and so on of that tradition. It would be advantageous to understand how those outside the tradition are to be viewed by those inside the tradition. Also, if ever caught in the belief of others being unworthy, how was that overcome?
- Promoting non-dualism and mutual interdependence. Many of the world's major religious traditions promote the separation of the believer from the non-believer, women from men, adults from children, the educated from the illiterate, the saved from the non-saved, the observer from the nonobservant, the body from the mind, the legitimate from the illegitimate, the healthy from the sick, the living from the dying, and so on. If the hospital is to reclaim hospitality, and chaplains are to reclaim themselves as hosts, we should reflect on how duality can undermine hospitality and how the privilege and power of being a chaplain undermines the awareness of mutual interdependence.
- Demythologizing entitlements around who receives and deserves healthcare. In the United States, a capitalistic country that has enti-

tlement programs and often strives to reduce the cost of medical care, to make our hospitals hospitable toward trans patients, we need to examine the ways we create hierarchies around who deserves medical treatment. For example, if one holds fast to the belief that God created us perfectly, then no one would deserve medical treatment to change anything about the physical body. I have not heard one *reasonable* person say that God has created your mind perfectly, so you should not have your paranoia, schizophrenia, suicidal ideation, homicidal ideation, major depressive disorder, anxiety, etc. treated. If the mind, which is part of the body, can be treated, the body, which is part of the mind, can also be treated. Think non-dualistically. Demythologizing requires reasonableness, compassion, and humility.

- Demythologizing religious supremacies. When a patient enters the hospital, what is the most important aspect of who they are? I would suggest that initially, it is their pain, their disease, their disability. Medical professionals have to assess the health need and proceed to determine the medical solution, treat the person, and return the patient to their life. A hospital employee who does not support this necessarily reductionist approach, but rather dwells in religious righteousness, poses a risk to the reputation of the hospital as a place of healing. Even if the hospital is a healing "ministry" open to the public, a patient should be treated for their illness first, because, in the interest of civilization, people need to have faith that their institutions will not turn on them. The Trump-Pence administration is turning on transgender citizens and hospitals have been targeted as ground zero for this oppression.

- Williams, Owens, and Syedullah are African-American and queer. They embody two "outlaw" identities in a predominately white, hetero-normative country. Their identities inform their experiences, work, and encounters in their *Radical Dharma* campaign. Making hospitals hospitable for transgender patients will be aided by transgender leaders, be they chaplains, doctors, social workers, or people from other professions. The transgender-hospitality-transforming leaders should identify other departments in the hospital that will host chaplains and their colleagues for conversations about compassion, the US Constitution, religion-based executive orders, Supreme Court cases, the Conscience and Religious Freedom Division of Health and Human Services, and so on.

• Chaplains may not be known to organize themselves into communities of resistance, but it is time to consider consolidating the power
of loving and compassionate spiritual caregivers to transform the
consolidation of hatred, ignorance, and delusion regarding those targeted by governmental laws and policies. It is important to note that
many human beings have a tendency to scapegoat a vulnerable
minority when they become afraid. Love and compassion should be
offered in ways to help people move through their fear.

Radical Dharma, though it is about transforming racism in predominately
white sanghas, and is not written by transgender people about making
hospitals hospitable, illustrates how, through looking deeply at oneself and
claiming the ways we have participated in delusion-making and perhaps
even injustice, we can begin helping others recognize their own collusion.
It is the awareness, humility, and acknowledgment that our thoughts and
behaviors may have negative consequences that inspires change, not guilt
and shame. The *Radical Dharma* methodology is a deeply engaged, rela-
tional practice that does not require identification as a Buddhist practitioner, is not limited to race issues, does not require the leaders to be queer
or of African descent, and is not limited to the sangha. This is a transformative model that goes beyond religion, race, and spiritual community.

In addition to this methodology, I add inspiration from Brita Gill-
Austern, a Christian pastoral theologian, about forming an "active solidar-
ity" while "shocking" the system. In her article "Engaging Diversity and
Difference: From Practices of Exclusion to Practices of Practical
Solidarity,"[15] she offers a possible movement-practice paradigm for pro-
tecting vulnerable patients from religious-based discrimination. Gill-
Austern suggests that solidarity with the oppressed can happen through
three movements and practices, including,

1. First Move: Know Home. First Practice: Self-Examination,
   Confession, and Repentance

To know home means, in part, "to know and own our familial home,
cultural home, economic home, and our faith home. We need to know the
landscape of where we have been dwelling all these years and bring it to
full consciousness."[16] Self-examination, confession, and repentance
includes acknowledging our delusions about ourselves, confessing our
own spiritual poverty, and "confront[ing] and expos[ing] the idolatry of

gluttonous consumption that teaches us to choose things over people."[17] As we contemplate cohabitation, as Judith Butler invites us to do, we also contemplate knowing home.

2. Second Move: To Make Pilgrimage. Second Practice: Constructive Engagement with Otherness

We need to leave home to become "dehabituat[ed] from [our] accustomed environment."[18] In Making Pilgrimage, one must enter into "constructive engagement with otherness."[19]

3. Third Move: Returning Home. Third Practice: Partnering with Others

Pilgrimages often end when one returns home after having had constructive engagement with otherness. Having first examined oneself, confessed and repented, one is ready to partner and be in solidarity with others. Gill-Austern, williams, Owens, and Syedullah share common attitudes and practices that can potentially help shock a health care system out of the practices of religious exclusion and the delusion of a false sense of ownership and the compulsion to capitalize while building solidarity with transgender patients.

Can knowing one's own story of awakening from religious discrimination, along with mindful meditation, engagement with the world, honing insight in a retreat, being in dialogue, non-dualism, renouncing the myth of meritocracy and the myth of Christian supremacy, shocking and deconstructing the system, and advocating for relinquishing a false sense of ownership and the compulsion to capitalize, help protect Americans from demagoguery in health care settings? Would williams, Owens, and Syedullah's method be made stronger if they were to add the practice of confession and repentance? In *The Way of the Bodhisattva*, Shantideva writes:

> Blindly I have brought forth wickedness,
> Inciting others to commit the same.
>
> I have taken pleasure in such evil,
> Tricked and overmastered by my ignorance.
> Now I see the blame of it, and in my heart,
> O great protectors, I declare it!

> All the evil I, a sinner, have committed,
> The sin that clings to me through many evil deeds;
> All the frightful things that I have caused to be,
> I openly declare to you, the teachers of the world.[20]

Confession and repentance are the ways of a bodhisattva and a Christian. Can williams, Owens, and Syedullah's view of non-dualism enhance Gill-Austern's view of mutual interdependence? Through meditation practices in "Equalizing Self and Other" [21] and "Exchanging Self and Other,"[22] solidarity comes through empathy and compassion. Consider this stanza from Shantideva:

> Strive at first to meditate
> Upon the sameness of yourself and others.
> In joy and sorrow all are equal.
> Thus be guardians of all, as of yourself.[23]

I believe non-dualism and mutual interdependence go hand-in-hand because they are similar, if not the same, but this must be tested within spiritual care professional organizations and health care settings. Here is a vision of how that might look with respect to trans patients:

- Chaplains and their partners can help other health care workers understand what it means for health care workers to be engaged with people who are not like themselves in every way, and how that engagement promotes their spiritual and ethical growth and
- Chaplains and their partners can advocate for health care workers taking personal time for spiritual and/or ethical renewal with regular retreat practice and pilgrimages.

Widening the field of pastoral and spiritual care for transgender hospital patients requires patience and determination. Leaders must gather, strategize, reach out, find departmental partners for dialogue, engage colleagues in real conversations, demythologize, deconstruct, become more law literate, deepen spiritual practice, including practices in humility, engage in acts of solidary, and advocate for hospital staff to have time off to reflect. We must move from a private to a public practical theology that includes religious freedom law literacy and lobbying.

A concerted effort in *Radical Dharma* solidarity can have ripple effects throughout hospitals and beyond if leaders choose to apply their method outside their institutions. It is important that transgender chaplain leaders and their colleagues lead and be engaged in the dialogues, but in the absence of these leaders, or if there are not enough transgender leaders to do the work, compassionate leaders who are cisgender will have to suffice, bringing attention to the fact that the United States needs more transgender chaplains to make liberation from religion-based transphobia a reality.

Pacific School of Religion in Berkeley, California is working to make this vision a reality through a Transgender Religious Roundtable. The aims of this initiative include:

- To create and provide spiritual and religious resources for transgender people that affirm them wholeheartedly;
- To support trans-identified clergy and other faith leaders in all the uniqueness and ordinariness of their vocations and life-paths;
- To encourage religious communities, churches, seminaries, and other faith-based organizations in their affirmation of the full dignity of people of all genders;
- To bear witness to the spiritual issues of transgender people in the wider LGBTQ community;
- To mobilize religious communities and faith-based organizations as advocates for social justice for transgender people in the wider society.[24]

Theological schools and chaplain clinical training sites like Sojourn Chaplaincy at Zuckerberg San Francisco General Hospital and Trauma Center, are responding to the educational needs of transgender people in ministry.

NOTES

1. Nhat Hanh, Disc 2.
2. Nhat Hanh, Disc 3.
3. Nhat Hanh, *The Ultimate Dimension*, Disc 3.
4. Ibid.
5. Ibid.
6. Seed is a term for an essence that lies within the unconscious, or store consciousness.

7. Nhat Hanh, *The Ultimate Dimension*, Disc 3.
8. Shantideva, *The Way of the Bodhisattva: A Translation of the Bodhicharyavatara*, Padmakara Translation Group, trans., Shambhala, 2003.
9. Ibid., 35.
10. Ibid., 50.
11. Ibid., 63.
12. Ibid., 98.
13. angel Kyodo williams intentionally uses lower case letters to spell her first and last names.
14. Not all predominately white sanghas are racist, but these authors, and many others including Larry Yang, Ruth King, and myself, have found it remarkable how in our experiences, our sanghas did not provide safe spaces to discuss the suffering of racism.
15. Brita L. Gill-Austern, "Engaging Diversity and Difference: From Practice of Exclusion to Practices of Practical Solidarity" *Injustice and the Care of Souls: Taking Oppression Seriously in Pastoral Care*, eds. Sheryl A. Kujawa-Holbrook and Karen B. Montagno, Fortress Press, Minneapolis (200) 29.
16. Ibid., 37.
17. Ibid., 38.
18. Ibid., 40.
19. Ibid., 41.
20. Shantideva, 43.
21. Ibid., 180.
22. Shantideva, 187.
23. Ibid., 123.
24. Transgender Religious Roundtable. https://clgs.org/our-work/transgender-religious-roundtable/ (Accessed October 30, 2018).

CHAPTER 6

Conclusions and Recommendations

Abstract The political context of religious freedom law enforcement in health care settings, in addition to hateful rhetoric and physical violence against transgender people, requires health care employees, specifically hospital chaplains and educators, to expand their traditional roles from bedside spiritual companions to practical public theologians. This expansion includes shocking the hospital system that has become "chilled" by religious freedom enforcement, becoming literate about religious freedom law, becoming active lobbyist against discrimination in the name of religious freedom, and becoming culturally competent. Buddhist-Christian dialogue can inspire and support the womb visualization practices and Buddhist gathas in the Thich Nhat Hanh tradition. It is recommended that chaplains and spiritual care professionals implement the practical and trans-culturally-specific instructions called "Special Considerations for Pastoral Care in Health Care Settings" by consultants Bradley and Metrick of Elements Consulting.

Keywords Clinical Pastoral Education • Elements Consulting • Gathas • Jake Bradley • Nate Metrick • Thich Nhat Hanh

© The Author(s) 2020   123
P. A. Yetunde, *Buddhist-Christian Dialogue, U.S. Law, and
Womanist Theology for Transgender Spiritual Care,*
https://doi.org/10.1007/978-3-030-42560-9_6

The US transgender community remains vulnerable as long as the reli
gious freedom to discriminate is protected by the US government.
Chaplains, pastoral counselors, and spiritual caregivers, many of whom
work in public hospitals that serve transgender citizens have an opportunity to shift the national conversation from the right to religious discrimination to the responsible exercise of religious freedom. It appears, however,
that pastoral and spiritual care professionals are not yet literate enough in
religious freedom law, to effectively advocate for responsible religious
freedom practices. Religious freedom law education for chaplains in seminaries, divinity schools, and Clinical Pastoral Education can ameliorate this
deficit, and, if warranted, organizations like Human Rights Campaign can
add spiritual care departments to their indexes for locating quality spiritual
care for transgender patients.

Public hospital chaplaincy departments are largely led by chaplains affil-
iated with Protestant-Christian traditions, but Buddhists are emerging in
the fields of clinical pastoral and spiritual care. Given the interreligious
nature of Clinical Pastoral Education, more Christians and Buddhists are
working together for the benefit of those in health care treatment.
Buddhist practitioners willing to engage in Lady Mahamaya-inspired visualization practices such as Mystical Transcendental Transsexuality, creating
the conditions for experiencing Relative Realm Gender Fluidity, may offer
their Christian interreligious dialogue partners practices that can inform
St. Paul's nongendered Christ consciousness and transform hatred against
trans people into love of their kin. Their interreligious dialogues can
include topics related to Paul O. Ingram's four-part framework of
Conceptual Dialogue, Conceptual Dialogue with the Natural Sciences,
Buddhist-Christian Socially Engaged Dialogue, and Buddhist-Christian
Interior Dialogue. I am suggesting that the Buddhist-Christian dialogue
within spiritual care clinical contexts also include law, psychology, government, and religious anthropology. Why increase the complexity of already
complicated conversations? Because a society that is hostile toward transgender people contributes to depression, anxiety, suicidal ideation, sui-
cides, and violence against our trans kin. Thich Nhat Hanh's unique
Buddhist teachings have much to offer Christians, especially his discus-
sions of Lady Mahamaya. I call his visualization practice a Mystical
Transcendental Transsexuality that promotes Relative Realm Gender
Fluidity. Christians who believe, as St. Paul believed, that in Christ there is
no male or female, may appreciate visualization practices that allow binary
gender constructs to dissolve into Christ-consciousness in the here and

now. Our bodies do not radically change through this practice, but our gendered self-concepts may loosen, potentially expanding our ability to empathize with transgender patients, or trans chaplains with cisgender patients. Mindfulness of the body should include the remembrance that we all have a unique blend of hormones and chromosomes and that hormonal changes occur throughout our lives, changing our experiences of feeling "male" or "female."

The ability to empathize will be the power that drives chaplains toward being in political solidarity with transgender patients and shocking the hospital system into returning to its roots in hospitality. *Radical Dharma* solidarity as practiced by queer African-American Buddhists williams, Owens, and Syedullah, combined with the movements and practices of Gill-Austern's Christianity, can go a long way toward transforming hospital culture from the inside out. The shock is not intended to feel good; the objective is to offer something radical and immediate such that new life is given to the dying. What are some practical steps spiritual caregivers can take to provide hospitality to those targeted by our legal and political systems? Think of the Parable of the Good Samaritan as The Parable of Our Collective Survival.

The Parable of Our Collective Survival involves four people. In this parable, we learn that the priest (who I call the anointed) sees the vulnerable man and keeps walking. The Levite (who I call the pious) also sees the vulnerable man and keeps walking. It is surprising to think that those who are considered spiritually pure would be the ones who would act heinously toward the vulnerable by depriving them of mercy, but that is exactly what religious freedom to discriminate laws attempt to do. These laws provide a legislative mechanism for the anointed and pious to organize themselves against a perpetually despised and vulnerable group of people. The Parable of Our Collective Survival teaches us that the Samaritan (who I call the despised) and the helpless (who I call the vulnerable) teach the anointed and the pious what it means to live according to higher purposes. Higher purposes, beyond being a good neighbor to one vulnerable person at a time, ensure our collective survival through the process of mutually desegregating civilization. Mutually desegregating civilization is when the despised responds to the vulnerable out of compassion and mercy despite the negative labels each have carried, and the vulnerable allows the despised to be who they truly are—responsive to others' needs—and accepts their compassion and mercy. When Jesus tells the lawyer to do as the Samaritan did, he is inculcating in the lawyer the capacity to give birth to the bodhisattvas and buddhas within himself and those in need. Herein lies a microcosmic example of the macrocosmic existential situation we all share.

In the late 1980s, I was visiting my cousin Damon (not his real name) in California. He was engaged to be married to Lois (not her real name) who seemed very kind and engaging. We were talking about the earthquake we had experienced the previous night. Lois told us about a time when an earthquake hit while she was working in her office. As the earth shook, Lois and her two male colleagues ran to their designated safe place and held hands underneath a desk as they feared for their lives. Lois lamented, while telling the story, that on what might have been her last day on earth, she was holding hands with a gay man and an atheist. She wondered how God could have put her, a good Christian, in that position. Lois, the pious and also vulnerable, could not bear the thought that the despised (who were also vulnerable) had comforted her (the pious) in her vulnerability. To be comforted in our vulnerability is the path to salvation. Let's tell The Parable in a way that inspires all people to see that they are part of the collective and are all vulnerable thus must care for the collective, and be cared for by the collective, in order to survive as civilized human beings.

With the introduction of the Department of Health and Human Services Office for Civil Rights Conscience and Religious Freedom Division (CRFD) subjecting vulnerable hospital patients to discrimination on religious grounds through the threat and potential loss of hundreds of millions of dollars to hospitals, chaplains must become more aware of religious freedom laws in order to protect themselves, their colleagues, patients, and the public health care institutions they serve.

Clinical Pastoral Education (CPE) programs are at risk. First, their application for interns and residents does not clearly state in writing that CPE involves intense and prolonged interreligious dialogue on spiritual care matters. Second, the application does not have an alternative dispute clause. With the reality of CRFD, an alternative dispute clause could serve to put the applicant on notice that interreligious disputes on care within the bioethical domain of a hospital will be resolved within the hospital. I am making the argument that although the First Amendment applies to all US citizens, because our reality is interreligious cohabitation, the patient's care in the hospital, not an employee's exercise of religious freedom, is the priority. Places of worship are where one's exercise of religious freedom is the priority. Keeping public hospitals in mind, with patient care as the priority over the exercise of religious freedom, especially the religious freedom to discriminate, public hospitals (and other health care organizations) are the places where we enact mutually desegregating civilization. Is there anything the despised and the vulnerable, in relationship with one another, can do to invite the anointed and the pious into the process of mutually desegregating civilization?

The despised and the vulnerable can teach us how to disobey, resist, and transform oppressive laws. They can show us how to make economic systems more transparent and participatory, revive humanism in religion, and intentionally moderate our desires in order to make room for another's desires to manifest. We learn how to cohabitate.

Sullivan says,

> Today CPE has no particular expressed religious identity, focusing rather on the praxis-oriented professional development of the minister of any tradition—or none. CPE care is theorized using a fusion of the student's own theological tradition, behavioral and social scientific knowledge and methods, and a "multicultural" perspective of respect founded in popular constitutional ideas.[1]

Sullivan does not state what the constitutional ideas are, but my 2018 research with chaplain educators hints that these constitutional ideas may be freedom and equality. Survey responses demonstrated a high literacy rate regarding the First Amendment and a high rate of tolerance for difference. Chaplain educators draw on a variety of resources to help their interns and residents cultivate compassion for those outside each student's religious group, including the intern's or resident's own religious traditions and practices, the US Constitution, chaplaincy organization's professional code of ethics, their own values, professional standards of care, hospital expectations, and other resources. When asked, "How do you cultivate compassion for those outside your religious group?" chaplain educators answered, advocacy, ethical commitments, meditation, prayer, selfless service, and a list of other methods. Though it appears that chaplain educators value freedom and equality, two constitutional ideas consistent with the universality of the "ministry of presence," chaplain educators tend not to talk with their students about the First and Fourteenth Amendments. Their methods for cultivating compassion do not include a reading of the US Constitution, in whole or in part.

If these surveys are an indication that spiritual care professionals throughout the United States are largely unaware of laws and legislative processes and not inclined to offer their expertise to legislators, care professions should examine the perils to them and those they serve and decide whether or not becoming politically involved should be a part of what it means to be a spiritual care professional. Can we take what works in private and make a civilizing impact publicly? It is time for chaplains to come out of the closet!

I believe Buddhists and Christians work well together in chaplaincy situations because we have shared values in personal transformation away from the compulsions and habits of self-gratification and toward selfless service. Christians teach the values of justice seeking and advocacy; Buddhists train in the understanding of no self and practices of exchanging self for other. Christians and Buddhists have much to offer one another.

Thich Nhat Hanh encourages people wanting to live mindful lives to practice the gathas he learned when he first entered monastic life, gathas derived from the *Avatamsaka Sutra*. Nhat Hanh says, "When I wrote the gathas for using the telephone, driving a car, and turning on the computer, I did so within the tradition that I inherited from my teachers. You are now one of the inheritors of this tradition. Composing your own gathas to fit the specific circumstances of your life is one wonderful way to practice mindfulness."[2] Unlike the teen-aged Nhat Hanh, I was 40 years old when I first encountered Buddhism and Nhat Hanh's special flavor of it. I am one of the inheritors of that tradition. Now, 18 years later, I have composed my own gathas to fit the specific circumstances of our transcleansing, hospital-as-site-for-discrimination culture under the Trump-Pence administration.

GATHAS FOR SPIRITUAL CARE FOR HOSPITALIZED TRANSGENDER PATIENTS

On the Morning of the Workday

As I awaken
coming to my senses that I am still alive
I dedicate this day to the well-being of all I encounter

Entering the Hospital

Mindfully walking into the hospital
I smile to all I meet

Dedicating my compassionate energy
For the transformation of suffering

Preparing to Meet the Transgender Patient

Mindful of my body
I breathe in to relax my body
I breathe out to relax my body
To bring a calm presence to those in need

Mindful of My Body

Mindful of my body
I know I am not my body
Mindful of my bodily forms
I know that all forms are empty and impermanent

Visualizing Lady Mahamaya

Visualizing Lady Mahamaya
I have the capacity to birth buddhas and bodhisattvas
With this spaciousness
I believe we can awaken together

Greeting the Patient

Mindful of our surroundings
I assess if conditions are comfortable for them
Seeing the patient
I say hello and tell the patient I come with well wishes for their health

Asking the Patient What They Need

Mindful of my mind
I search for an agenda
Finding an agenda, I drop it
I open, like a flower, to what the patient needs

Asking for Permission from the Patient

Listening deeply to the patient's need
I reflect on myself as a generous resource
If I have the ability to give
I ask the patient if they want to receive

Bringing the Love of a Parent

Aware of the mystical teachings of no birth and no death
I refrain from imposing these beliefs on others
Like a loving parent would
I celebrate the new birth of this patient

Embodying Hospitality

Aware of the deluded politics of discrimination
I bring non-dual consciousness to bear
Embodying Indra's Net
We reflect each other's light

Checking Connection

Conscious of our mystical interdependence and interpenetration
I know not everyone believes or feels this connection
Checking in with the patient
I connect with them where they are

Taking Leave

Mindful of being hospitable
I remember I am also their guest
I greet with open arms and
I leave with palms together (as in, with a mind of prayerfulness and gratitude)

I believe practicing "Gathas for Spiritual Care for Hospitalized Transgender Patients" can go a long way toward transforming our biases, prejudices, and even transphobia, but chaplains also need the practical advice that already comes from the best practices for caring for transgender patients. Nate Metrick and Jake Bradley of Elements Consulting (team@elementsconsulting.org) have compiled a list of best practices they call "Special Considerations for Pastoral Care in Health Care Settings.[3]" Some of those special considerations include:

- Don't ask specifics about a person's body or medical history related to gender. Don't make assumptions about a person's body parts.
- Be especially sensitive if someone is having treatment for, or concerns around, a health issue that is seen as gender-related. If it becomes necessary to refer to someone's body parts that are often gendered, ask people what names they use for their body parts, and encourage other caregivers to use those (if the person is comfortable having you talk to other caregivers about that). Use gender-neutral language for body parts as often as possible (e.g., refer to someone's "chest" or "crotch").
- Be sensitive to someone's potential needs for additional privacy and modesty. Offer extra blankets or an extra layer of gowns or pajamas.
- Advocate for trans people to retain access to and use of their appearance-related items such as wigs and prosthetics. These are not luxuries or vanity materials. They are often needed for a person to feel safe in their body and to be themselves.
- If someone comes out to you, ask how they'd like you to handle that information. Don't assume that their medical staff do or don't know. Ask which family members and friends who might visit or whom you might encounter are aware.
- Ask how they want to be referred to in front of others. Know that a person's needs could vary for different people and contexts, and this is about their choice and safety!
- Don't out anyone, ever!
- Offer to support a person in coming out to or stating their needs to medical staff or friends and family. Offer to be present with them if they are intimidated by other staff or visitors.

As it relates to faith/religious/spiritual concerns, Bradley and Metrick suggest:

- Ensure that transgender people have access to rituals and rites of passage for their religion or faith path (baby blessings, bar/bat mitzvah, coming of age ceremonies, etc.) that are not gendered, or which affirm their gender self-identity.

- Be aware of faith communities and other pastoral care providers who can be counted on to be affirming, safe, and respectful.
- Be aware of the various kinds of abuse and alienation some LGBTQ people have experienced from religion, and be prepared to help someone process that or find them a trustworthy clergy person who can.
- Don't advise someone to stick with the body that God gave them, or that they need to learn to accept their body or the gender they were assigned at birth.

Other important considerations include:

- Seek to see and understand all the different aspects of identity (gender, race, sexuality, faith, etc.) and oppression (racism, sexism, ableism, heterosexism, etc.), and how different forms of identity, oppression, and privilege intersect with each other. (In other words, a person's gender or gender status does not "trump" all the other parts of their identity—they are a whole person, whose various identities all inform each other and co-create each other. Keep in mind, for instance, that gender is raced and race is gendered—that the concept of each thing and how it is perceived and expressed is informed by the other.)
- Don't make excuses for your ignorance, or your failure to understand a person or treat them with respect and compassion. (Apologize if you've hurt someone's feelings, and ask what you can do to be safer for them.)
- Don't expect one trans person to represent an entire group of people. (e.g., don't ask one trans student to account for the whole trans community. If you're asking a question, know that you're asking them about themselves only.)
- Be honest about what you know and what you don't. Do your own education. Practice with people to gain better skills.
- Join with other allies, and seek support and feedback, and hold each other accountable.

The cultivation of mindfulness through writing and practicing gathas, coupled with the embrace of best practices, helps create safe and hospitable places for people to heal. As Bradley and Metrick have suggested, let's not make excuses for our ignorance, or our failure to understand, or our failure to treat people with respect and compassion. Pichette, Bradley, and Metrick are experts on religious experience and spiritual care for trans people. Attacks against trans people continue. Our governmental systems of checks and balances are being undermined, and the clarion call for "religious freedom" (ironically in one of the most religiously free countries on the planet), is an opportunity for wise resistance to tyranny and solidarity with trans people who are oppressed by our federal and state governments. Professor, activist, and TV host Melissa Harris-Perry, a theologically-educated political scientist informed by feminist and womanist scholars, demonstrates how the integration of theological and political academic disciplines can be applied to a liberatory public theological-political discourse. She is an inspiring and fierce example of how chaplains can publicly advocate for transgender people. Chaplains need to know more about religious freedom laws to avoid being agents of tyranny so that we become public practical theologians advocating for freedom from tyranny. If Sullivan is right about the role of chaplains and our practices in presence and universality, let's be bold and share with others how we live authentically while simultaneously bracketing our beliefs while we promote civilized living. If we come out of our closets of relative safety and risk shocking systems from the chilling effect of fear, applying williams, Owens, Syedullah, and Gill-Austern, we do our part in this world in a bigger and bolder way. This is how we can best be in solidarity with the transgender community. Spiritual formation through chaplaincy training, Nhat Hanh Lady Mahamaya-inspired Mystical Transcendental Transexuality that promotes Relative Realm Gender Fluidity, something akin to St. Paul's nongendered heaven, and Buddhist-Christian dialogue holds promise for the deepening of empathy for our capacities to at least temporarily alter our concepts of fixed gender identities and capacities. Chaplains are no longer just prayer partners; we are becoming the ministers oppressed people can count on to create safe spaces through becoming religious freedom law literate, shocking the hospital system when necessary, re-imagining parables to include the collective, using visualization to loosen the grip of overidentifying with gender constructs, being in solidarity with the oppressed, and thereby creating safe spaces through collective engagement with the political process.

Postscript. At the time of writing (April 8, 2020), President Trump's impeachment retaliation, even though he was acquitted, is being felt. In the midst of the COVID-19 crisis, he fired the inspector general responsible for shining light on the whistleblower's claim. COVID-19 has infected more than 1,444,000 people worldwide and over 83,000 have died. In the midst of this devastation, Trump also fired another inspector general responsible for COVID-19 oversight. By the time this book is published, these numbers will have increased exponentially, and our government will not have the independent, inspector general oversight we once had. The light on government is dimming. My August 2018 Freedom of Information Act request regarding religious exemptions from providing health care in hospitals remains unanswered. Is the subject of religious discrimination against ill transgender people still relevant in the face of a pandemic? Consider this. Refusing, on religious grounds, to treat patients with COVID-19, be they transgender patients or not, runs the risk of spreading the virus, sickening thousands and killing thousands, including health care providers and other first responders. We must ask ourselves, "Is helping to spread disease at home and abroad a religious practice protected under the US Constitution? Does the government have a compelling interest in protecting the health of its citizens? If so, why did President Trump fire the inspector general (otherwise known as "watchdog") tasked with overseeing how money would be spent to deal with COVID-19? Without a world government, do citizens of the world have an ethical duty to protect one another? Is President Trump's threat to defund the World Health Organization (WHO) a prudent move?" Our health care landscape is changing radically and dramatically. The US military has been deployed to build massive temporary hospitals on military ships, in parks, barracks, and convention centers. The New York National Guard was ordered to seize ventilators from private hospitals. Cruise ships have offered to turn their vehicles into makeshift hospitals. States are competing against each other for resources. States are competing against the federal government for resources. We are buying ventilators from China. Taiwan is donating masks. Morgues are public charnel grounds. Our economies are devastated. Pandemic health care is a very public, global matter that requires the attitude of universalism, not religious exemptions. May this universalist attitude, embodied in the best of our chaplains, pastoral counselors, and other spiritual caregivers, our Compassion Corps, inform and transform our movements toward hospitality, co-habitation, empathy, compassion, loving kindness, nondiscrimination, religious freedom law literacy, and human rights advocacy.

NOTES

1. Sullivan, 126.
2. Nhat Hanh, *Present Moment, Wonderful Moment*, 3.
3. Jake Bradley and Nate Metrick, email message to author, January 29, 2019.

BIBLIOGRAPHY

"A Date Which Will Live in Infamy": FDR Asks for a Declaration of War. http://historymatters.gmu.edu/d/5166/. Accessed August 28, 2018.

About the Trevor Project. https://www.thetrevorproject.org/about/#sm.00001 mirt4urfgdpos19r0ro6y6yz. Accessed January 13, 2019.

Advancing justice through intersectional scholarship and engagement. http://ajc-center.wfu.edu/wp-content/uploads/2012/12/syllabus-black-religion-political-thought-spring-2013-ajc.pdf. Accessed March 3, 2018.

American Psychiatric Association. *Desk Reference to the Diagnostic Criteria from DSM-5*. Washington, DC: American Psychiatric Publishing, 2013.

"Americans Are Poorly Informed About Basic Constitutional Provisions." https://www.annenbergpublicpolicycenter.org/americans-are-poorly-informed-about-basic-constitutional-provisions. Accessed January 10, 2019.

Bowie, David, Pat Metheny, and Lyle Mays. "This is Not America." *The Falcon and the Snowman* soundtrack. https://en.wikipedia.org/wiki/This_Is_Not_America. Accessed September 21, 2018.

City of Boerne, Petitioner v. P.F. Flores, Archbishop of San Antonio, and United States, 521 U.S. (1997).

Cleary, Thomas. *The Flower Ornament Scripture: A Translation of The Avatamsaka Sutra*. Boulder: Shambhala Publications, 1993.

Clinical Services. https://www.bmc.org/center-transgender-medicine-and-surgery/clinical-services. Accessed August 28, 2018.

Compelling-State-Interest-Test Law and Legal Definition. https://definitions.uslegal.com/c/compelling-state-interest-test. Accessed September 3, 2018.

"The Discrimination Administration." https://transequality.org/the-discrimination-administration. Accessed September 12, 2018.

© The Author(s) 2020   135
P. A. Yetunde, *Buddhist-Christian Dialogue, U.S. Law, and Womanist Theology for Transgender Spiritual Care*,
https://doi.org/10.1007/978-3-030-42560-9

"The Economic Cost of Overly Broad RFRAs." https://www.americanprogress. org/issues/lgbt/news/2016/02/04/130566/the-economic-cost-of-overly-broad-rfras/. Accessed September 12, 2018.

Employment Division, Department of Human Resources of Oregon, et. al. v. Alfred L. Smith et. al. 110 S.Ct. 2605 (1990).

Finnegan, Joanne. "As complaints trickle in, protecting workers' religious rights could cost health industry upward of $300M in First Year," *FierceHealthCare*. https://www.fiercehealthcare.com/practices/protecting-workers-religious-rights-cost-healthcare-300m-donald-trump-hhs-roger-severino. February 6, 2018a. Accessed January 12, 2019.

———. "New HHS office that protects religious rights has received more than 300 complaints from health workers," *FierceHealthCare*. https://www.fierce-healthcare.com/practices/more-than-300-complaints-health-workers-hhs-religious-rights-donald-trump. February 22, 2018b. Accessed January 12, 2019.

Gill-Austern, Brita L. "Engaging Diversity and Difference: From Practice of Exclusion to Practices of Practical Solidarity." In *Injustice and the Care of Souls: Taking Oppression Seriously in Pastoral Care*, edited by Sheryl A. Kujawa-Holbrook and Karen B. Montagno, Minneapolis: Fortress Press, 2009.

Green, Erica L., Katie Benner, and Robert Pear. "'Transgender' Could be Defined Out of Existence Under Trump Administration." https://nytimes.com/2018/10/21/us/politics/Transgender-trump-administration-sex-definition.html. Accessed January 9, 2019.

Guan Yin, information about. https://simple.wikipedia.org/wiki/Guan_Yin. Accessed September 9, 2018.

H.R. 1308—Religious Freedom Restoration Act of 1993. Congress.gov. https://www.congress.gov/bill/103rd-congress/house-bill/1308/text. Accessed October 3, 2018.

Hanh, Thich Nhat. "All in One, One in All." https://sites.google.com/site/tnhdhamma/Home/test-list/all-in-one-one-in-all. Accessed August 28, 2018.

———. "Avatamsaka Talk." https://tnhaudio.org/tag/avatamsaka-sutra/. Accessed August 21, 2018.

———. *Awakening of the Heart: Essential Buddhist Sutras and Commentaries*. Berkeley: Parallax Press, 2012.

———. *Chanting from the Heart: Buddhist Ceremonies and Daily Practices*. Berkeley: Parallax Press, 2007a.

———. *Cultivating the Mind of Love*. Berkeley: Parallax Press, 1996.

———. "Dharma Talk: The Power of Visualization," *The Mindfulness Bell* #38, Winter/Spring 2005. https://www.mindfulnessbell.org/archive/2015/06/dharma-talk-the-power-of-visualization-2. Accessed September 6, 2018.

———. *Going Home: Jesus and Buddha as Brothers*. New York: Riverhead Books, 1995.

———. *Living Buddha, Living Christ*. New York: Riverhead Books, 1995, 2007b.

————. *Present Moment, Wonderful Moment: Mindfulness Verses for Daily Living.* Berkeley: Parallax Press, 2006.

————. *Touching Peace: Practicing the Art of Mindful Living.* Berkeley: Parallax Press, 1992.

————. *The Ultimate Dimension: An Advanced Dharma Retreat on the Avatamsaka and Lotus Sutras.* Compact disc, Sounds True, 2004.

Hanh, Thich Nhat and Daniel Berrigan. *The Raft is Not the Shore: Conversations Toward A Buddhist-Christian Awareness.* Maryknoll, NY: Orbis, 2001.

Harris-Perry, Melissa. "A letter to Phil Bryant about putting rights in God's hands." http://www.msnbc.com/melissa-harris-perry/rights-mississippi-now-subject-religion. Accessed March 3, 2018

————. "LGBT Advocates Need Public Progressive Faith." http://religiondispatches.org/melissa-Harris-perry-lgbt-advocates-need-public-progressive-faith/. Accessed March 3, 2018.

————. "Progressive Bible Study." https://www.thenation.com/article/progressive-bible-study/. Accessed March 3, 2018.

————. *Sister Citizen: Shame, Stereotypes, and Black Women in America.* New Haven, CT: Yale University Press, 2011.

Health Care Equity Index. https://www.hrc.org/hei/search/massachusetts/boston-medical-center. Accessed September 6, 2018.

HHS Announces New Conscience and Religious Freedom Division. https://www.hhs.gov/about/news/2018/01/18/hhs-ocr-announces-new-conscience-and-religious-freedom-division.html. Accessed September 3, 2018.

Hospital, etymology of. https://www.etymonline.com/word/hospital. Accessed August 27, 2018.

How many adults identify as transgender in the United States. https://williamsinstitute.law.ucla.edu/research/how-many-adults-identify-as-transgender-in-the-united-states/. Accessed September 12, 2018.

Hurley, Lawrence. "U.S. court rules for Trump on transgender military limits." https://www.reuters.com/article/us-usa-court-transgender/us-court-rules-for-trump-on-transgender-military-limits-idUSKCN1OY1BI. Accessed January 9, 2019.

Ingram, Paul O. *The Process of Buddhist-Christian Dialogue.* Cambridge: James Clarke & Co./The Lutterworth Press, 2011.

Katcoff v. Marsh, 582 F. Supp. 463 (E.D.N.Y. 1984), 4.

Larson, Kristin. Union seminary president complains on MSNBC about male-led Catholic Church. https://juicyecumenism.com/2012/02/24/union-seminary-president-complains-on-msnbc-about-male-led-catholic-church/. Accessed March 3, 2018.

Masterpiece Cakeshop, Ltd., et al., v. Colorado Civil Rights Commission et al., 584 U.S. (2018).

Melissa Perry, personal website. https://www.melissaperry.com. Accessed March 2, 2018.

Mendieta, Eduardo and Jonathan Vanantwerpen, eds. *The Power of Religion in the Public Sphere*. New York: Columbia Press, 2011.

Minority Quotes. Brainey Quote. https://www.brainyquote.com/topics/minority. Accessed September 12, 2018.

New HHS office that protects religious rights has received more than 300 complaints from health workers. https://www.fiercehealthcare.com/practices/more-than-300-complaints-healthworkers-hhs-religious-rights-donalt-trump. FierceHealthCare. Accessed January 11, 2018.

October 2015 Ratings: MSNBC Up Double Digits. http://www.adweek.com/tvnewser/october-2015-ratings-msnbc-up-double-digits/275722. Accessed March 2, 2018.

Phillips, Layli, ed. *The Womanist Reader*. New York: Routledge, 2006.

Pichette, Aurora Jade. "Passing Through Divinity: An Anti-Oppressive Window into Trans Women and Religion." M.SW. thesis. Ryerson University, MSW, Toronto, ON, Canada, 2013.

"President Donald J. Trump Proclaims January 16, 2018, as Religious Freedom Day." https://www.whitehouse.gov/presidential-actions/president-donald-j-trump-proclaims-january-16-2018-religious-freedom-day/. Accessed September 3, 2018.

Reasonable person, definition of. https://legal-dictionary-thefreedictionary.com/Reasonable+person+standard. Accessed September 3, 2018.

Religious Freedom Restoration Act, 2017. http://ncsl.org/research/civil-and-criminal-justice/2017-religious-freedom-restoration-act-legislation.aspx. Accessed September 12, 2018.

Shantideva. *The Way of the Bodhisattva: A Translation of the Bodhicharyavatara*. Padmakara Translation Group, trans. Boulder: Shambhala Publications, 2003.

Spiritual care. Boston Medical Center. https://www.bmc.org/services/spiritual-care. Accessed August 28, 2018.

State Religious Freedom Restoration Acts. http://www.ncsl.org/research/civil-and-criminal-justice/state-rfra-statutes.aspx. Accessed September 12, 2018.

Sullivan, Winnifred Fallers. *A Ministry of Presence: Chaplaincy, Spiritual Care, and the Law*. Chicago: The University of Chicago Press, 2014.

Thompson, Frank Charles, ed. *Thompson Chain-Reference Study Bible, New King James Version*. Indianapolis, IN: B.B. Kirkbridge Bible Company, 1997.

"Trangender Religious Roundtable." https://clgs.org/our-work/transgender-religious-roundtable/. Accessed October 30, 2018.

"Trump Rolls Back Transgender Bathroom Guidelines For Schools." http://fortune.com/2017/02/22/trump-lgbt-transgender-bathroom-guidelines/

U.S. Constitution-Fifth Amendment. Cornell Law School. https://www.law.cornell.edu/constitution/fifth_amendment. Accessed October 5, 2018.

Walker-Barnes, Chanequa. *Too Heavy A Yoke: Black Women and the Burden of Strength*. Eugene, OR: Cascade Books, 2014.

"What is Gender Dsyphoria." https://www.psychiatry.org/patients-families/gender-dysphoria/what-is-gender-dysphoria. Accessed October 29, 2018.

Yetunde, Pamela Ayo. "Black Lesbians to the Rescue! A Brief Correction with Implications for Womanist Christian Theology and Womanist Buddhology." *Religions*, 2017a, 8(9), 175, 1, September 2017.

———. Chaplain Educators and Religious Freedom Curriculum Survey, Fall 2018, Harvard Divinity School Post-Doctoral Fellowship project.

———. Pastoral Counselors Religious Freedom Pre-Survey, Summer 2017b.

———. Religious Freedom for Chaplains Survey, Summer 2017c.

Index[1]

---

[1] Note: Page numbers followed by 'n' refer to notes.

CPSIA information can be obtained
at www.ICGtesting.com
Printed in the USA
LVHW081417310520
657056LV00018B/1278